Incranium

Jon-Pat Myers

Published by Burning Books, 2021.

While every precaution has been taken in the preparation of this book, the publisher assumes no responsibility for errors or omissions, or for damages resulting from the use of the information contained herein.

INCRANIUM

First edition. April 22, 2021.

Copyright © 2021 Jon-Pat Myers.

ISBN: 979-8201736224

Written by Jon-Pat Myers.

A few moments

I stand directly under the milky way. At least it seems so as it divides the sky neatly in two and I'm looking up at the halfway line. I can make out the Southern Cross only due to my familiarity as it is almost hidden in the misty light from the billions of heavenly bodies that emit and reflect light.

I walk out towards the ocean and am struck by the unmistakable smell of kelp and fresh spray from the little waves that crash and undulate amongst the rocks. The air is crystal clear and frozen and not a single wisp of a cloud obscures the star studded darkness overhead.

Its a moonless night.

I wander a little further and feel the inside of my skin begin to tremble with the windy onslaught of cold air. Slowly my eyes become accustomed to the light or lack thereof and I realize how much glare there actually is from the city across the bay. It casts its tired light on the rocks and if there was no water I could easily be fooled into thinking that I am standing in a place stellar and far away.

Two nutcases drive past on the road nearby on motorcycles and I shake my head and do the quick calculation that they must be experiencing a wind chill factor of around minus 17. And I wonder almost out loud what planet they may be from.

My eyes become more accustomed and I see the reflection of the street lamps in the distance upon the fragmented water. The breeze is cutting. Penetrating right through my fortifications and chilling me to the bone. I tremble with a subdued epileptic violence.

I have just changed my clothes which was a necessary task enabling me to maintain a semblance of respectability in the morning when I will meet the people once again.

Its beautiful...

The sounds of the waves, the smell of the kelp, the feel of the grass and pebbles that crunch underfoot as I stroll.

An aeroplane appears from behind the mountain like some kind of spaceship. Low and noisy. Going straight towards its designated landing strip with landing lights on high and blazing. Nervous passengers in its bowel. The entire craft is reflected in the water as it is precariously low and barely clears the breakwater as the pilot guides the cumbersome avian machine to a safe landing and I can almost hear the sigh of relief coming from relieved travelers securely belted up within the fuselage.

I try to regulate my breathing and relax into the cold but its a win lose fluctuation. My hands are numb and my ears and nose burn in the stinging wind.

I take a second out to think of the poor folk and I pity them.

Snuggled up duvet clad in front of their heaters and wall hung, oversize plasma screens in their designer homes that keep them happily numb.

I feel a sense of pity yet I realize that I have to respect their choice irrespective of how I feel about it.

Every sinew. Every muscle. Every bone. Every blood vessel. Every pore. Every part of my being screams out in exultation and I realize how fortunate I really am.

I see the lights of the cars in the distance and watch as they approach each other unknowingly and then dim their lights at the last moment and then re-engage the brights once they have passed.

The beacons on the peaks of the surrounding hills flash and the distant lighthouses blink their binary warning to ships and approaching planes.

I am just awed at how fortunate I am to be alive right now.

Its not all carefree...

I keep a vigilant watch for Police cars on the road as I dread the intrusion and barrage of questions. Who are you? What are you doing? Why are you here? Where is your passport? Do you mind if we have a look in your vehicle? Etc, etc, etc..

When I look towards the road I notice the dim blue glow of my little gas stove gamely battling the breeze and slowly accomplishing its nightly mission of warming up my instant noodles in my aluminium billy can that has provided such excellent service in the most adverse of conditions in the past. It hisses and bubbles in the darkness and I catch the hint of a scent of my meal. Liberally laced with herbs and spices and tasting better than the 15$ suppers that are so freely available in the center of the city.

The noodles are my lifeblood and provide me with the much needed calories that will burn up and heat me from the inside and cement up the gaping hole in my gut that is a constant reminder that it is now supper time.

My complete meal costs no more than 69 cents in total.

I watch the distant stars and planets twinkling away majestically and wonder if I am seeing light that has long, long ago left a source which is now dead and still makes its way across space to stimulate the cones in my eye and stimulate the galaxy within what is me.

Suddenly I become aware of the sound of traffic but am confused as its source is the mountain opposite. I soon realize that it is the echo of the sound of the engines of the ferry that connects the South Island with the North. I turn in the opposite direction to see that my hunch is correct and watch as the lights slowly make their way across the ice cold black. I think about the sea and all its mystery and wish I knew more about the creatures who live so close by but in a separate reality.

I look back towards the land and see the street lights and think that each one is representative of about 10 people who are all asleep right now or huddled, duvet clad in front of their heaters and extra large plasma screens.

I feel a sense of pity but understand that I have to respect their choice irrespective of how I may feel about it.

Golden oldies

Age creeps up on all of us and it seems that old people are the most creepupable since father time has made it almost all the way home with them.

Old people are usually depicted as being scatty, grumpy and of course...old fashioned. In many cases it's true but there are also oldies who are really cool. In my book they win the punk by default prize as they simply couldn't give a damn about current conventions and simply do as they like and say what they feel when they feel it. Besides those old bats have purple hair!!

Having a heart to heart with an old person can be a most disheartening event but usually, if one shows enough patience and tact, there is a whole lifetime of experiences to tap into and so the whole encounter can be a magical experience.

Consider that some old people today were up and kicking just a heartbeat after the Wright brothers did their first seemingly impossible flight. The amount of change that old people have seen in their lives is a world record as at no other time in recorded history has so much happened to so many in such a few amount of time...

In Israel I painted houses and some of the older folk who were either hell to deal with or were simply solid golden oldie material, actually had numbers tattooed to their hands or forearms. It wasn't exactly a conversational opener but you could see by the way they carried such weight that they had had life experience that was beyond anything I could readily understand. Older people still, were gassed in the first world war and were still pretty together enough to crack jokes about being so old that they now knew the difference between a stick up and a hold up!

Most young people wouldn't give them the time of day. Change happens so fast now that anything older than a few years is referred to as old school, but thats another story.

It always amazes me how some older folk talk about new technologies such as the cassette tape and computer with such a sense of awe and even a slight touch of fear. To try to tell them that most young people today haven't the faintest idea of what a cassette tape is or that the average kid can type at 3000 words a minute and cant actually wield a ballpoint pen is pushing the envelope a little. What some of them do have in common though is a distinct lack of concentration span.

Old people are cool though. I love the way they will shout into the phone when you inform them that its an overseas call.

Getting older must be weird. Your body starts to have a mind of its own and so does your mind. Each day you are treated to a new ache or pain or simply a sound in your knee which has no logical reason whatsoever. You get to feel like an old crone one minute and a little child the next, complete with diaper. You seem to become at ease with disease and in extreme cases you actually forget that you're suffering from Altzheimers. Doctors use you in much the same way as they would a lab rat if they're the caring type or conversely drug you to the gills to get you out of the way.

Our family has a pretty good record when it comes to aging though. My aunt went skydiving on her 70th or was it 80th birthday?? I'm not so sure..... my memory fails me. Anyway it was such a big deal that the news got hold of it and featured a short clip of this skydiving granny complete with Van Halen blasting "Girl you really got me now.." as the soundtrack! Well cool.. Her brother who is actually my father is just as rad. He now sports a metal knee and has lots of fun with airport security every time he goes through the metal detector. He is nearly 86 and a few years ago was a little embarrassed to admit that he hurt his thumb due to falling off his bike. He told the doctor that he fell out of bed as he couldn't admit that he was doing some geriatricks on his 18 speed mountain bike! Needless to say I sit here beaming with pride.

Old people have a lot to teach as I have said and to me they are the most underutilized resource in any and every society.

The "back room boys" era is long gone and its a pity. Back in the day it was possible for one individual to become a master of not only his trade, but a host of overlapping ones as well. The skill these old guys had is just phenomenal. Boat builders and mechanics were used to making their own tools, servicing their machines and creating their own parts out of raw materials. Today with such specialization its a thing of the past. In fact in many places it contravenes union law. Encroachment I believe its called. Don't fix it. Call the fix it guy. If you do, you are doing that guy out of a job and so its a no no and its a shame.

Some years ago I had the rather unique opportunity to fix up some of my folks friends houses as they were ready to move out into smaller premises and were putting their houses up for sale. I would go and stay on site and naturally had some very interesting conversations with my hosts Most, if not all of these people were my folks oldest friends and had known me long before I was born so being the sensitive and tactful young man that I was, I asked them "OK, so,..you're old and at the end of your life and I am young so what advice would you give me? Do you have any regrets?" I asked the same question to 7 people and their answers went something like this. "I wish I had learnt to play a musical instrument. I played when I was younger and always wanted to." "I wish I would have spent more time painting. I wasn't much good but its something I always wanted to do." "Oh boy! I wish I had been a carpenter! I always loved the smell of the woodwork shop." All of the answers were like that except for one guy who wouldn't have changed anything. He had a house the size of downtown Chicago and you would drive for 20 minutes through a forest before coming upon a mansion which was his service quarters and then another 20 before you reached his "garage" where he kept some of his classic cars in vacuum packed plastic bags and in a sealed temperature and humidity controlled room. He had had about 16 failed marriages and was a grumpy old bastard when he happened to be in a good mood and for the rest of the time he was even grumpier. Needless to say I added a generous sprinkling of salt to his comment.

As to the other more honest answers I learnt a valuable lesson. Not one of those people even mentioned not receiving a promotion, bonus, a great car or anything along those lines. Every single bar one of them regretted doing something that concerned personal development. Not cash, fame or any of the more expected things, but dormant talent. They didn't want to be professionals or break a world record. They simply wanted to improve something in themselves that gave them a sense of achievement and self satisfaction.

To me it was a revelation. They had reached an age where they weren't taken in by slimy politicians which they all uniformly derided, they were all pretty confused and by no means convinced in terms of so called accepted spiritual practice, they were all disgusted with the capitalist system (bar one!!) and they were more interested in tending their gardens than in the world at large and it really gave me an added sense of perspective.

The last time I ventured in those questionable waters was when I asked an old Mexican whilst I was in Mexico. "Hey Amigo! You're old. What can you tell me?" with my beamingest Gringo smile. He took quite some time to consider and then replied "You can buy you time or you can sell your time!" and continued sitting contentedly on his porch watching the day pass him by.

I thought it was dumb at the time but lately I have begun to wonder.

My back yard

Its weird...It only took a few days and bam!...... I'm alone.... One minute I was in the kitchen with ten people all jockeying for the same frying pan and then..in a few short days I'm one of only three people here!

The nights are the most noticeable at first...no lights in the TV room...none in the kitchen...no smells of cooking or burnt toast..... no condensation on the windows...just an eerie silence.. I become aware of the sound of my footsteps on the boardwalk and somehow they seem louder than ever. Disturbing the quiet before them with each tramp up towards where many people used to be only days ago.

The trees show their age too and the strain of the season just gone. Oranges and browns dot the landscape and I am most drawn to the lime green and yellow trees that I ride my bike past on a carpet of undisturbed leaves.

Its quiet at night. Peaceful.

Some evenings are light and crispy with an immaculate view of the sky overhead. Others more insulated as the cloud covers and mist drops in the early mornings. When its frosty the mornings are clear and ice cold and then transform the surroundings into a sun basked wonder all in high resolution focus and clear as a bell.

I inhale as deep as possible and never want to give the spent air back to the atmosphere that surrounds me so closely.

The lake has her moods. Some days mirror like and others with a steady lapping and clip breeze accompaniment. The tones and colors chop and change as the day has its moments. Evenings are spectacular as the high altitude clouds light up in bright pinks to wish the sun a good nights rest. The lake in kind responds with a respectful array of tones that can only be created with water and so adds its unique contribution to the early evening symphony of cloud and sky.

The mountains surrounding the lake are all different yet linked by contrasts in background silhouette.

Towards Manapouri the distinctive shape of Titaroa looms up in the background against a silver crystal sky. No clouds obscure the peak and the subtle variations in white just manage to be distinctive enough to those with the eye for it. In the foreground the "water mountain" shape coming in from Rainbow Reach creates the transition from last horizon line in to the middle ground. From the control gate through to Brod bay the observer is reminded of the friendliness of the fruit flies on that side of the lake shore and unconsciously scratches at a hard won bite from visits before. As usual the air is alive.

Its rained once or twice. Mushrooms have pooped up everywhere and some like in little colonies. I look at them and I imagine a dome house colony in the forest and where I would place my house.

My room is small but warm and dry. I have a good bed and far too much stuff for such a small space.

My window faces East and I get good morning light when there is and a fairly good view of the forest.

Each evening the Southern Cross is clearly visible as is Orion.

The small forest that borders on the park is quiet and covered in pine needles. There is this undisturbed carpet of brown and I half expect to see a Deer jumping out from behind a tree.

Small Fantails fly around my head and perch on branches to peer at me.

I walk up the ridge to get a view of the Murchesons and don't have to go far before I stop and look at the cloud enshrouded peaks in a respectful silence. They're beautiful.

The thing that is missing of course is the people.

People come from around the world and end up together in a place for a few months and in some weird way get to know each other quite well and then in a flash the time comes when you have to say goodbye and part ways. Its an occupational hazard as a traveler that you will meet people and have to say cheerio at some later stage, I mean OK!

Thats obvious! But it doesn't make it any easier when it comes to the crunch. Saying goodbye always hurts.

Next morning I'm up before the cleaner...then I realize..I am the cleaner! And ..I'm late!

Rush over the ice covered deck that sparkles in the early morning sunlight. The only absence of normality is the lack of foot and bootprints that usually disturb the clean sheet of frosty cover that loves to linger in the shady spots. Slide down the slope and skid into the cleaning room, grab my supplies and I'm off!

No toilet is safe from my super duper extra special wonderfully good for the environment too... squirty goodie. Or my mop! I have an adult size one too and boy does it get to those tough bits that ordinary mops just don't get to.

I'm an absolute expert when it comes to mirrors. How many wonderful hours have I not spent in front of it admiring its lack of spots. Mirrors are the only real truth. They reflect only what is shown. No more. No less.

Dump two good sized loads into the washing machine just for luck and then off again to make beds to the usual perfection. Each room is a work of art and then to the laundry which is My Domain!

No sheet is in the wrong place or towel left untidily folded. I'm a veritable master of the subtle art of doing the laundry. My workstation is spotless!

Lunch is a downplayed affair with only half an hour to do the necessary, but then its paid so what the hell! Instant noodles to the rescue again.

Afternoon is left over for my fold fu session. After which a brief tidy up and the world is once again mine for the taking.

Now its time to be creative...first with lunch and then with the days main activity which could be the usual...TIDY UP! The damn place or just organizing files on the computer.

I write projects a lot and so am constantly busy with writing and sending off the mails and so on.

If I am up to par with my workload then I may ride the bike to see a good sunset or go for a short walk to the jetty and look at the Murchesons as the sun goes down.

Most of the time I just miss my kids and fantasize about our future meetings together and their visits here when I eventually have the house and so on.

The rest of the time is devoted to writing or keeping my audio diary. Sometimes writing and recording songs. Quite often I will sketch or go out and take some pix which I'll add to a project or file or whatever.

I have recently been working on a bird made out of old bicycle frames that I have stripped and welded together. The whole thing is pretty much there and I have only to do the face at this point, then do some strengthening and paint and done!

So change is a constant and people come and go. The sadness of saying goodbye is overshadowed by the memories of good times and great people.

And they last forever.

Passive fist

I'm an insomniac.

For those of you that don't know, that's someone who doesn't sleep like a brick. Or briquette for that matter.

My usual ploy is to go & go & go until I simply have to collapse and then begin to wrestle with the pillow and sheets with the single minded hope that I will make it down the long and winding road to dreamland before the first light of dawn.

Last night was much the same and as usually happens; exactly at the moment when I cross the moat into the impenetrable castle of slumber I hear the unmistakable drone of the lone Mosquito on the prowl for fresh blood.... Mine!

Falling into the familiar trap of outright denial, I take cover beneath the covers only to emerge a few minutes later from the well perspirated sheets to embark on the early morning search and destroy mission.

It isn't long before I spot him for the first time. I adopt the correct ninja stance and stealthily make my way toward him......concentrate ...and ..POUNCE!!

I miss dismally

. There is no doubt, this is one fast boy!..

I am no pushover either and have read my fair share of military strategizing classics. The art of war by Sun Tzu comes to mind and I search for the appropriate passage to deal with the problem at hand." The one with the biggest gun usually wins" somehow emerges from the depths. I struggle to trace the source.

All that fades into the background as I spot him again and decide that it's time for the "Fat nappy surprise!" It is something that I don't often resort to but it is obvious that this guy is good. I launch the nappy and he is gone. Not so, the yellow dripping splotch that will take some explaining at a later stage. No matter as I have lost him and begin the wait. I realize that this is no ordinary quarry. Definitely well trained. Al Kaida possibly, but impossible to tell as the sleek filling machine is flying with an unmarked fuselage. I ponder the Art of War for some time longer and then move on to the classic of five rings, and I get the idea…What if I wrap my training Samurai sword in sellotape with the sticky side exposed? I know it's unorthodox and not exactly in accordance with the Geneva code an' all that but Sun Tzu and his buddies never had to deal with heat sensors and night vision and besides the whole idea is to be flexible in battle. It doesn't take me long and I am actively in pursuit with the innovative weapon clutched in my clutches.

It takes a while but patience pays off and I spot him. I approach and prepare to strike. Unfortunately I miscalculate and catch the curtain on the backswing and as I strike I hurl it across the room to alight upon the TV which I manage to save from crashing down by employing my cat like goalkeeping skills and dive across the bed and pin it to the stand before any real damage is done. Miyamoto Musashi would not be too chuffed and I cringe as I imagine him turning in his grave. To add insult to injury the Midnight Ranger defies personal danger and does a victory roll right next to my ear. I instinctively swipe at him and succeed in slapping myself so hard across the ear that I am still unable to hear and it's now two days later. The singing has abated somewhat though.

I am not yet beaten. In fact I now resort to the standard weapon of all warriors throughout the ages. RAGE!..... I am gonna kill the bugger!

Somehow the word Banzai drifts into my amply spaced skull and I vaguely remember all those stories from the old fella's at the Moth club were I used to go drinking while still underage. They used to talk all the time about flushing the enemy from their holes by using flamethrowers and my porous mind makes the quantum leap. I go straight to the bathroom and grab the first air freshener I get my hands on and then it's off to the kitchen to acquire a lighting device. I am now fully armed and strut around like De Niro in Taxi driver.."Speaking to me?!!.. Huh!.. Huh!" I see him and don't hesitate. ..Fffsssssst!

HA!...But the Ha is on me as I watch the white foamy spludge drip down my lighter carrying fist like shaving cream with the distinctive post poo aroma that we all know so well. In my haste I grabbed the non flammable spray and feel as foolish as home made sandwich at Mc Donald's.

I gather my well scattered resolve and contemplate the Russian method. Last time I used it though I ended up electrocuting the cat so I am a little reluctant. What you do is place a flashlight in the freezer and wait. As soon as the bastard enters you slam the door and simply go to sleep. Hypothermia takes care of the rest. It's neat, effective and very well suited to the lazy assassin or political tyrant although it's not too cool if you know what I mean. But then the killing business has never really been too cool. The Mafia used to "Ice "people but that only lasted till the slang term became passé and then they did stuff like

" snuff, whack, put on the cement boots or dress in the wooden pajamas"

I wait the obligatory seven breaths laid down in the Hagakure and then go for broke.

I am ashamed to admit that this vampiristic midget beetle is simply out of my league and so will have to call in my shock troops!

I slink over to where my wife is sleeping soundly and whisper the one word into her ear...Mozzie!

The transformation is miraculous. Instantly eyes are ultra wide. The tracking system is automatically activated and homes in on the target. No tiny crack is safe for the enemy to try to hide. Running is completely out of the question. I watch transfixed as she becomes vertical and proceeds to walk/stalk directly over the kitchen table without as much as a downward glance Magically she doesn't disturb a single item from last nights meal. No clinking fork or clunking plate. SILENCE!..In a straight line she makes her way to the opposite side of the room and strain as I might I am blind to what she is able to see/sense.

ZAP!.. Faster then the eye can see she has struck before I am aware of it and holds up her blood splattered palm with the evil grin of the triumphant. I am reminded of the Native American Indian in his heart feeding frenzy at the new kill, but realize that it is a little over dramatic and I am virtually dreaming as I stand. She washes up, smiles and goes straight back to sleep without a hitch. I can only look on with a mix of awe and unadulterated admiration.

I am too hyped up by the hunt at this stage and decide that it wouldn't be proper to hit the sack without somehow honoring my recently fallen adversary. I grab the trusty axe and play a Hendrix style version of the last post and say a few words.

I learn an important lesson by the events- It is far easier to get someone else to beat up the bully. It's poetic in a sense and quite close in essence to the not engaging in battle concept of the venerable Sun Tzu.

Enough!...I make my way to the mattress I call a bed and do my best to find a comfortable position to dispose of another days consciousness.

I am well down the road to the land of dreams and as I am entering the gates of the city.....I hear the feint yet ominous buzzzzz...

Thick skinned

I'm thick skinned!

So they don't tell me..I'm unable to take the hint. So they don't tell me too.

That's the whole thing with hinting. Nobody really says anything. No one stands up to be counted and take responsibility for what they should be saying but don't. It's not PC! I HATE.. PC!. Being politically correct is simply game playing nonsense and an excuse for being too chickenshit to say what you mean. It's a social affliction and the foundation for all forms of office politics.

It stems from a basic lack of security. Security in the sense that not only are you unable to say what you mean but most people are totally unprepared to accept straight talk. It is a stepping stone to outright violence in some societies and thus avoided at all costs. The problem with that is that most of us walk around in a daze. We tend to guess at best, what our true standing in our social circles could be and have the constant uncertainty that goes with the knowledge that you are guessing. The outcome quite often is complete self delusion. In a way, it is a self preservation mechanism, as it is far better to make yourself believe you are cool than to know you're just an average twat. The other side of the coin is to let other people know (through the grape vine of course!) that it is they that are twats and so, by elimination you tend to move more toward the cool side of the scale. Hence, hinting. It's like planting a seed and watching it grow. Direct and obvious approaches are sometimes, well, just that. Obvious and direct. There is no appeal to our innate sense of game playing. Innuendo's....what an amazing tool for the manipulative. There are many others. All subtle and nasty in a strange kind of way.

The main appeal of the whole hint game is that you remain unaccountable due to the lack of clear evidence that you are in fact being a bastard or bitch to some poor, albeit deserving soul. Also of course it has been the age old weapon of the weak, yet intellectually nimble, against their brawny and physically stronger counterparts.

All in all, it sux in my book.

Now I am not advocating the complete absence of tact. Much less the brash verbal bludgeoning of the chronically insensitive. But rather the cultivation of a climate in which straight talk could be a scalpel that allows us as the social creatures that we are, to cut through the crap. To add color to the grey areas that provide us with the opportunities that are open to misinterpretation and thus a lead us to further conflict.

Conflict can be good, as is obvious in our many and varied forms of competitive sporting activities. The difference being that there is always the concept of sportsmanship that acts as an undershirt for the dinner coat of honour. A code of ethics is required and it is not analogous with our current concept of Political Correctness. Treading a fine line I know but it all comes down to the mentality and insight of the person who is adhering to the so called code. With a sense of dignity and consideration for the other, we will be able to make the transition into the no mans land of direct communication.

Without fear.

Because , if there is mutual trust and respect, then this type of communication can take place as a logical outcome and not as some kind of contrived attempt at barrier breaking.

I am thick skinned . When people begin to hint I become tenfold more so. The usual progression is to start dropping the proverbial bricks and I become more thick skinned. It's juvenile I know, but I am insulted by hints that are directed at me.

On the other hand it is really difficult for me to say something straight out to someone when I know it may be taken in the wrong way or be damaging to the listener. There is the conflict always, and contrary to what one may expect it is usually more difficult to tell something disagreeable to someone that you care about. The irony is that the whole point is that by talking straight we should become closer to each other as a society. How so? Well, by talking straight I mean to tell the truth. Unpleasant things as well as positive things. Take for example the most used and abused phrase in the world: "I love you" It can heal and kill. Say I love you to a friend and you could weld the relationship of a lifetime. Say it to a fellow worker at the office party and you could destroy the relationship completely. The opposite is to tell someone that you are angry with them has the possibility of ending a potential conflict before it really begins in earnest.

The ego....It's an animal in its own category. PC and hinting and insinuating and so forth are all children of the ego. The delightful little devil that everyone carries around wherever they may go. Truth becomes an ego destroying tool and is frowned upon. The illusion or delusion is destroyed and it's just not PC to do that kind of thing!

I have an enormous respect for what little I know of the North American Indians. They used to sit down in a circle and everyone had their say. Without fear of discrimination. Each had a turn to speak his mind and the Chief would listen to all and speak last. When he spoke he would speak as one that is a listener and the decisions he would make by and large were what he would consider to be in the interests of the tribe at large. This in itself is not what was remarkable. What was to me the most telling thing was the fact that the rest of the participants would abide by his decision whether in favor or not. Sometimes this would mean their deaths, but it was a point of honour to follow through with what the Chief had decided. That is magical.

In today's world, when a leader makes an unpopular decision then a referendum is held, and while the political jockeying continues, nothing gets done and the people suffer.

The irony is that the founding fathers of the United States molded their democratic constitution on a template that was comprised of many of the key concepts implemented by the Native American Indian s in their societies. Freedom of speech being just one.

I hear the groan from those that are still awake at this stage and concede that it's a pretty tough line for me to take on what is basically an accepted form of gossip. Well, yes! It is a tough line but it is something that is indicative of a much greater ill that has befallen our current society and that is the crippling effect of the tolerance of vicious verbal violence. No matter in how subtle a form. It is a disrupting force to the potential harmony in human relations and a major stumbling block in our evolution toward the seemingly unattainable goal of being able to live together on one planet.

But then what do I know?

I'M thick skinned!

Ruksbi

Rugby! Perhaps you have heard of it? It's an interesting game played by large humans whose knuckles drag on the ground as they walk.

It's become a very popular sport worldwide and is played by Argentinians who are too large to play football and eat lots of steak. Italians play it and their bulk derives from steak and pasta washed down with wine for breakfast. Even Japanese play it which is a very scary thought given that they have the bushido code going for them and they commit hari kiri when they lose which is good for the second team players who will always get a chance to play. Their pronunciation is great too. Rukabi as in wasabi, and almost as hot.

All around the egg shaped globe the sport is gaining popularity and there seems to be no stopping the juggernaut invading gymnasiums in every nook and cranny of rugbydom.

Some countries have known about it for a while already and it can be said that certain countries have a 'Rugby mentality' To contrast, take for example the wussy footballers who fall down at the merest suggestion of their hair going out of place and writhing on the floor in theatrical agony whilst said coiffure is restored to its usual plastic like consistency before the game can be resumed. This is a football mentality and suits mostly Latin countries and English poofs who whine and bitch at any given opportunity about anything at all. When a goal is scored it absolute pandemonium! The scorer is so consumed by their own brilliance that even fellow members of the team are brushed aside during the victory celebrations. Rugby mentality isn't quite as histrionic although the game does have its riske' moments especially during scrums and other forms of close bodily contact. A game for 'real' men one might say? Which at times make even the most depraved Vicar squirm with homoerotic squirmitude.

Countries with rugby men tality would have to be led by New Zealand. To give an example; There's a guy who has just run through a forest fire and cut a hole in a frozen river to swim underwater in sub-zero temperatures for 2km without breathing to emerge on the other side and run headlong into a snake infested barn that's also on fire to rescue a puppy stranded on the top floor. Of course he emerges unscathed and when asked how he does such a heroic thing the answer is simple 'ah no worries mate! just doing me job!" Same goes when he scores the winning try. No dramas, just turn around and jog back to take his position and continue with the game.

Due to the uninteresting nature of this blatant display of boringness, international teams now employ a full time theatrical coach to teach players how to express emotion after bull dozing the opposition and passing the try line with ball in hand.

Now one may wonder, which countries are better suited to playing rugby than others and a wonderful wonder it is to wonder about. No wonder it comes as a complete shock to discover that Russians have not yet discovered the game! Everyone knows that you get out what you Putin but fact is that the entire rugby playing world is in cahoots with each other and pays the international press inordinate amounts of cash to keep rugby a secret from the Russians.

They were made for the game!

Now, Russians are not normal. They themselves consider themselves superhuman as their flights to space without oxygen, spacesuits or any form of sustenance proves. They consider themselves wussys just for having to fly in a spaceship and would prefer a tank if they could get it to fly. They have tried.

If they discovered rugby they would dominate the game for ever. Teams would be sent to Siberia to train stark naked with bears. The forwards would scrum against fully loaded tanks, on ice, whilst being fired at by drunken coaches with machine guns and still win the ball. The world doesn't stand a chance.

Now the crazy thing about Russians is that they are under the false impression that they invented the hairstyle known as the 'Mullet'

Its common knowledge in the rest of the world that this stylish head decoration was invented in Brakpan by people doing time in the local jail. The reason is simple. Being homophobic by nature and not wanting anyone to get close enough to their behind to cut their hair, prisoners resorted to cutting their own. Problem being that only a tiny mirror in the cell wouldn't allow the auto hairdresser to be able to see the back and in so doing leave it to grow out. Hence the resultant style and made complete by a very heterosexual moustache.

The irony is that Brakpanians and Russians are practically indistinguishable from one another. If you put some Rohypnol in their Klipdrift and Vodka respectively and transported them to each other's town and made sure they kept their mouths shut, no one would ever know they were from another place and time. Twenty years could go by and they would just be thought of as quiet guys and therefore liked by all and never suspected.

The Russians would make Rugby compulsory just like they do for martial arts, genocide and chess at schools. Entire government agencies would be set up to study the game even further than it's been studied by analysts all over. They would employ strategies never before thought of much less attempted due to their super humanity. And they would dominate the world for as long as it's inclined to spin.

Future Rugby players would be selected before birth and genetically modified much as they are now but much better and wouldn't even have to take steroids or go to gym. They would become bored with mere mortals and begin playing amongst themselves and bring the game as it's currently known to heights never before imagined.

It's a serious issue.

Just as the game draws ordinary folks into the spiritual realm by encouraging them to get on bended knee and pray to the Almighty just before the whistle blows, so will Rugby played by Russians transform the sporting world into an arena for peacetime conflict resolution like no other sport before it.

So be warned! Under NO CIRCUMSTANCES WHATSOEVER are you to let slip or even hint at the games existence within earshot of any Russian or friends of a Russian, because if you do...

We are fucked!

Unsung

Contrary to popular misconception it is not the movers and shakers who institute changes in this world. Well not entirely, there are the exceptions. The true innovators who influence the current of human affairs are quite often unknown to the world at large and only to a small number of privileged folk who hold these individuals in the highest esteem.

I refer to them as the Unsung Heroes.

There are many and I will just choose some at random.

So....Who invented the light bulb? I look over the mass of confused faces and stop at the nerd who informs me."Thomas Edison. Sir!" (I added that just to feel important!) And I bellow back at the quivering wretch. NO! WRONG!

Thomas Alva Edison gets the credit but the real man behind this and a whole bus load of inventions is a man by the name of Nikola Tesla. Now I am not surprised to hear that you have never heard of him and to those smarty pants out there who think I'm full of it I say. Bugger off!

Nikola Tesla was a remarkable man. He worked as one of an even larger bus load of specialists who "aided" the aforementioned Mr. Edison. The difference being that he was smarter than all of them put together including the even aforely mentioned Mr. Edison.

Tesla was a new immigrant to the States and whilst working for Edison he soon rose to prominence as a person with extraordinary abilities. For two years or thereabouts Tesla slogged it out and whatever he came up with was of course claimed by Edison as his own and it resulted in extreme jealousy on Edison's part and understandable frustration on Tesla's. The two clashed regularly and the animosity became so great that Tesla eventually left and Edison vowed that his name would never be recorded in Scientific history and actually spent most of the rest of his life toiling away to make sure that this would in fact be the case.

Tesla worked from a small shed of sorts and eventually held more than 200 patents that provided the groundwork for many of the succeeding inventions such as Radio and Television to mention just two. The outstanding point that I find most interesting is the fact that Tesla would be able to work out entire machines and so on completely in his head. He would then go to the technician's one at a time and say. OK..You make this part at such and such dimensions and You do this and so on. Each part would be manufactured and then assembled and on testing the machine would work!

He had some pretty far out ideas for his day and some pretty even far outer ideas regarding cosmic energies and such. Sad fact is that Edison being the politically astute person that he was managed in the end to make you and the rest of the world believe that he was the originator of so many things and seen by the scientific community for a genius. An astounding man he was but compared to Tesla he was a midget. And he knew it!

Second random choice is a gent by the curious name of George Washington Carver. Also known as the Peanut Professor.

Prof Carver was an African American who managed to discover an enormous amount of stuff about peanuts in a small shed that served as his lab and in a country and time when few if any Black people would be able to attend college.

I'm not sure of the amount but it's something like 200 different products that he managed to create out of peanuts as his raw material. Many things we use today are based on his initial research and he is not exactly unsung, it's just that no one really sings about him.

There are many characters such as Carver who managed the most extraordinary things despite severe hardships and adversity Maria Montessori being one albeit well sung.

Someone who did an enormous amount to shape our current world is a guy by the name of Buckminster Fuller or more commonly Bucky Fuller.

Bucky Fuller was highly esteemed by the Hippies who publicly stated that he was the only person over the age of 30 they could trust. His achievements are far too numerous to even start to put down here and his influence on future world shapers immense.

He was a guy much like Leonardo da Vinci in his diversity and the thing that mostly contributed to his relative unsungness was the fact that he was not really an institution qualified person and so could not be taken too seriously by the establishment at that time.

His most famous credit is for being the person who patented the geodesic dome which is quite ironic as it is something that he only really added to. The original domes were made by a guy way back in the 1920's

Bucky Fuller was remarkable in so many different ways and I will mention only two. First; He kept a journal of his life that he updated every 20 minutes! Second. He developed a method of sleeping for only a few short hours at a stretch and had to have numerous assistants a fifth of his age who struggled gamely in shifts to keep up with his irrepressible enthusiasm and energy. He was known for giving lectures for 18 hours straight in which no one would leave except to go to the toilet!

Today he is far more widely recognized and there is even a Fuller Institute set up to showcase his life's work and to continue with it.

There I will stop as there are so many invisible characters who through the ages have played a major role in shaping our current reality and get not a drop of kudos for it due to petty spite or simple political manipulation.

If it were up to me I would establish the Unsung Heroes Museum and finally provide the world with a look at some of the amazing people who worked all their lives to improve our current situation and never got the well deserved credit for it.

A serenade for the unsung.

Radio radio

Radio! Remember that? It was the square little planet with all the knobs that could be found in every house hold and stuck to the ear of every cool African who may not have owned his own bed but had a "transistor" and possibly a bicycle.

My friends father called it a "wireless" and I couldn't figure out why. My folks never threw ANYTHING away and so we had a whole shelf of them in the garage which had symptoms ranging from a loud hiss or low buzzz, to being nothing more than completely and utterly DEAD. So, I in my wise and youthful curiosity and daring took one and put a few shots through with the pellet gun it to see if it would explode but rather sadly it did not, then swiftly moved up a notch and simply threw it repeatedly against a wall until it had given up any vestiges of a ghost and quite literally spilt its guts to reveal that my friends father was way, way wrong. The mysterious little box was practically made out of wires! It confused me, but I knew better than to ask as I now shared that taboo with others like Leonardo and Michaelangelo....I was a dissector!! ...He was weird anyway...he would call a bicycle a push bike and takkies Val Doonicans!!

It fascinated me how the thing could work by "catching" invisible waves and spewing out sounds of all shapes and sizes. But it was a central part of all experiences growing up, along with all the PC that went with it. Children knew very well that when those pips sounded to announce the news and adults put on a stern face, that NO interruptions would be tolerated. NEVER ask a question, fart, clear your throat or breathe when Granma is listening to the Church Service and the Dominee is spewing forth words so scary and vile that you tended to get a little further out of immediate range and the room too, without showing disrespect ..or getting spittle on your shirt.

Those early days before television were in many ways much more interesting, with programs that were regulars with adults and children alike. The most famous one to my mind started at supper time and we all served ourselves as quick as possible and settled in as a request for salt or whatnot would be met by SSSHHHHH!!! from all participants,. Not a single second could be missed.

....."They prowl the empty streets at night...waiting with fast cars on foot....etc etc ....These are the men of.....Squad Cars!!!!" My whole body tingles with anticipation with the recollection. Each program was a roller coaster ride and it was never sure whether the crooks who tended to be from Brixton or Bez Valley, would get caught by th Warrant officers and Konstaaabils who were usually provincial rugby players as well and most certainly God fearing , real men...But invariably..after the last set of adverts..the boys in blue would risk their thick and duty bound necks to save the day and then the sentences were read out and we all felt and enormous sense of satisfaction at the knowledge that the streets were once again safe. I wonder how many avid listeners actually peeked through their windows or even rushed outside, gun in hand to help apprehend the baddies when they were escaping through the suburban backyards during the final chase scenes. "Squaddies" was the family favorite for sure.

On Saturdays my Dad would go to the bank and it would take ages and so I would sit in the car and program surf which wasn't allowed when adults or my older sister was around. I remember the Pip Friedman show and it was supposed to be hilarious based on the announcers plug, but for the most part I thought it was stupid. My sense of discernment grew with age and many hours of listening to the box and exploring the many stations in existence at the time. Being sick was perfect for it as you could spend the whole day listening to what you liked without interruptions from anyone. I would go to the huge music center in the sitting room and go through the programs and switch over to short wave and super short wave and even super duper shortest wave and tune in to nuclear submarines under 300 meters of ice at the North Pole and Radio Luxembourg which to my tiny little world view was the center of the known world, unbeknown to those with less hammier skills than I. It was here that I would tune into LM Radio and listen to "Underground" music without my folks knowledge and remember the jingle…"LM Ra-di-o..!"" It was a kind of secret club that anyone could join….

Sundays I would awake to my Dad blasting out the boiling toilet, extra special, super deluxe, Vindaloo blues on the Indian station and this would go on till way after breakfast with the family chior in the background adding the prerequisite and appropriate..OOOhs! and AAAhhs! On the subject of ethnic music…I remember going to Heidelberg to fetch my sister from boarding school and as it was a girls hostel I wasn't allowed in and so had to wait in the car. I was fumbling around with the tuning knobbie and stopped at an African station and just listened for a while. It was really strange music as, well, for one..I had an underdeveloped musical ear and so it was just a mass of music thrown at my grommet pierced timpanies and I couldn't make head nor tail or any other anatomical part of it such as the bass line or an instrument ..period. I was rudely interrupted by the red screaming face of one of the rugby jearsyed and beefy local boys who screamed…" MY LIEWE BLIKSEM!!!!!DRAAI AF DAI FOKKEN KAFFERMOESIEEEK YOU BLERRY ROOINEK VOOOR EK YOU EN DAI BLIKSEMSE RADYO VERMOOR!!!"

It was a short but emphatic end to my exploration into .."their" music. Pity though, as it is much later and with an intact although scarred eardrum that I immensely enjoy all kinds of music, African or otherwise.

One of my favorite programs was Darryl Jooste and Micheal Meyer's.."Take another Chance" No..it wasn't " Money or the Box!" It was a great and pretty whacky program with the both of them donning different accents and telling these bizarre stories that totally cracked me up. It was such a favorite of mine and I was so adept at mimicking the various characters accents that my Mom phoned them up and being the huge fan that I was, I was invited to attend a studio recording of their program at the SABC building in the center of JHB. It was amazing...I was given a short tour around the tiny studio and sat in the sound box while they did their thing and the engineer twiddles little knobs that were sound effects and had car doors slamming and water gushing down the stairs and all kinds of sonic magik. I was honored by being put into service and having to fetch coffee from the machine down the hall which I carried in a tape reel with the Styrofoam cups jammed into the spaces between the spokes. It was a great episode too and I remember that story quite well. A simple act of sending Philemon to fetch some coffee turns into a crazy flooding of the whole SABC building from a coffee machine that wont switch off and has the whole staff swept down Market or Commissioner street. I listened to the episode later that week and it was just great, complete with my favorite advert for "Botha's batterproof Bakkies!"

Some time later when I had a school trip to the studios my teacher was much impressed at my familiarity with the place ...largely due to the fact that the studio we visited was the exact same one!!

At one stage there was the regular afternoon programs like Jet Jungle that could stop a soccer game in mid kick when someones sister would shout out of the window.."Its started!" within seconds the street would be filled with wind...and all would be at home seconds later with a toast-an-jam in one hand and a coffee in the other listening to Petrocelli and the Panther who's name escapes me. Later it would be "Gruesome Gresh" and Springbok hits and more risky still would be hiding the radio before bedtime and then sneaking the earphone (one! Mind you) and plug it into the ear facing the pillow so Mom and Dad wouldn't see it when they came in to say goodnight. Radio under pillow of course and the program...My name is Adam Cain!! And another with a Yorkshire man named Frank Pybus...

Ooooh.... they were TOUGH!!!!

Just like the News and Kerk there were other things not to be messed with, such as THE RUGBY!!!! and BOXING!!! Rugby came first though even before Church/Kerk and my Mom would sit down with an open notebook and sketch the match as described with much emotion and intricate description by the one and only Gerhard Vivijee?? That guy was without compare. She had a whole code, with a symbol for a scrum, loose scrum, kicks, marks, the works. The page would fill up with scribbles and lines in black blue and red pen and could sell at Sotheby's for Gazillions as abstract art if the y could be found in amongst all the accumulated junk that my folks never throw..like dead transistor radios...

I had never heard of Pierrie Fourie but he became a national hero when he beat the crap out of the other guy against all odds and bad refereeing as we were passionately informed by the commentator who never missed a rabbit punch and could be trusted. I learned about a right hook and a cross and all kinds of technical stuff and imagined the brutal match blow for brutal blow which could have only resembled the real fight in the same way that a watermelon resembles a garden hose. But nevermind....it was exiting as anything

Technology marches on though and it was just before my teens when my sister showed me a really cool thing tat I wasn't supposed to tell the folks. At that age though anything you didn't tell the folks was cool but this particular thing really was...She took TWO radios and put them down facing each other and made me lie with my head between them and listen...WOW! I was amazed! "You know what thats called?" she asked...."Stereo!! Cool hey!" Man...it blew me away. It was music inside the middle of my head!!! Wow! Again. Later I would discover real stereo with the advent of the Walkman but I was addicted way before then.

My friend would always have better HI FI's than us. Our old wooden thing with the flap top was an antique but it never bothered us. It was a fixture and this could be because it was constructed by the same guys who built the Titanic and basically it was too heavy to move. Now I would go into Hi Fi stores and realise that the radio was referred to as a tuner, The tape recorder (cassette not reel to reel) was a deck and the record player was now a turntable.. the whole ting together with speaker that had woofers and tweeters cost more than our entire house and thats including the dogs and the view. It simply wasn't going to happen. The next best thing was to get blank tapes and give them to someone who did have a multiplex super wonderful machine and illegally tape LP's that were hired from the record library.

Yup. Technology marches on and soon we had the first test broadcasts of the new SABC TV and sooner even after that the color Salora sets and then TV as usual. Radio never went away though as it would always be there in the background at your local greengrocer or Motor mechanics workshop, but it would never be the same or have the same appeal. It was a wondrous time and a media source that stimulated the imagination like no other. The Internet is fine and I love it but lost is the sense of mystery and wonder. You couldn't very well send R mails now could you? Porn wouldn't happen as it makes for rather dismal radio and where would we be without Google and the Yube??? Clearly there has been progress of sorts.

...But I still look back and smile at the thought of being dead tired and forcing myself to listen to the last few parts of the late night shows before a severely coffee wired Rocko Erasmus would beam into my skull with the all night radio show of Radio South Africa..or was it Highveld Radio, or the English service who's idea of a cool audio experience would be to listen to the whole of Pagliachi ...again... or interview another master gardener who still explained things in feet and inches, or perhaps it was Springbok radio, Radio 5 or Capital radio..??

Well...actually it was all of them as broadcasts would stop at 12 midnight! And there would only be the one to listen to.....but by that time I was already tuned into the dream channel.....

Gaia

He awoke in the pitch black.

For some moments he lay blinking, not being able to discern the difference between eyes open and closed. The bed was warm and somehow he felt safe.

It was some time before the first feint light illuminated the edges of the window frame and he could begin to make out certain objects, hazily silhouetted in the room. His mind had become active and the last vestiges of a forgotten dream were dissolved by the encroaching conscious state.

He smiled to himself and anticipated the coming cold splash of air when he emerged from his womb like cocoon of cotton and wool.

Barefoot and naked he made his way to the bathroom to complete his morning ablutions and then after dressing quickly went outside into the wide open and patiently waiting day.

The Sun had not yet risen as he walked down the crunching gravel path to the water's edge close by.

His narrowed eyes sought the distant horizon.

The sky, as ever, resplendent in pink and purple and yellowing to announce the dawning of the solar cycle in the never ending spiral that is time.

The ocean spread out before him like a glistening carpet of grey blue interspersed with slivers of pure silver and gold was calm and serene. Endless, immaculate.

He stood motionless. Slowly dragging the crispy air deep into his lungs and exhaling with a sparkle in his eye and a Mona Lisa smile playing lightly upon his lips.

It was good to be alive!

A short distance away he noticed a small boat beached on the shore. It was blue with patches of green and seemed to glow in the early morning light and he wondered why he had never noticed it before.

He went closer to inspect this vessel that somehow emanated a sense of power and wellbeing at the same time. Its miraculous appearance left him in a state of mild awe and driven by innate curiosity he explored every nook and cranny within.

It was a most beautiful craft and he felt at once, a sense of kinship and familiarity with it. It was as if it had been placed there for his personal use by divine providence itself.

Suddenly in an almost impulsive manner, he took the boat and without hesitation dragged it out to the water's edge and launched it into the vast, wide and endless ocean.

He was afloat!

There was no looking back as he headed directly towards the waking Sun.

At first he rowed and then a short while later hoisted the sail. He was drifting with the current and followed whichever direction the wind would take him in. For the most part he headed toward the light and settled back comfortably to witness the rising of the Sun.

It was effortless. Nature plotted the course and he was content to adhere to Her wishes with absolute submission.

This continued for some time and soon the heat of the midday Sun forced him to drop the sail and use it as a makeshift shelter. He was now cooler and although adrift, didn't mind in the slightest.

He lay there. Dry and cool and content to simply be. Watching the sky and playing imaginative games with the shapes conjured up by the voluminous clouds overhead.

He was blissfully unaware when he drifted off to sleep.

He awoke some time later to the sound of the waves lapping up against the gunwale and was surprised to see that the light had faded and darkness was swiftly approaching.

He stiffened to the slight, yet persistently chilly breeze and wrapped himself in the sail to warm up.

Lying there he looked around at the uniform horizon and wondered which way land could be.

The smile had been replaced by the slight furrowing of his brow and he uncomfortably concluded that he was hungry.

It wasn't long before his growling stomach drove him to use his boundless ingenuity to create a makeshift net out of the sail and he tried for an extended time to capture something in it but was completely without success.

The cold had now penetrated his bones and with teeth chattering jettisoned the sail/net. He tried walking about whilst rubbing his body to keep warm but it wasn't very long before he realized the fruitlessness of the activity and sought a viable alternative.

What he needed was a source of heat and the only source strong enough to keep his internal temperature below a critical level that he knew of was fire!

He brightened up when he noticed the absolute abundance of fuel around him. The boat was made out of wood and surely there were some areas that he could gleam which could enable him to create the heat he needed.

He started with the mast. As he had no sail it would be ideal to use and so without further ado he dismantled it and in no time at all had created the spark that kindled the flame.

He was rapt.

Huddling over the dancing orange and yellow light he silently congratulated himself and basked in the radiated warmth.

Soon, however, his initial supply had dwindled and he searched for other sources.

He pried bits off here and there and stoked the flames till a small but rather healthy looking blaze was lighting up the entire area and he sat comfortably once more.

That was when disaster struck.

A tiny spark popped out into space, flew over his head and landed behind him and this created a small flame of its own.

The cool breeze that caused him to sit a little closer to his heat was at the same time it fanning the semi accidental creation he had inadvertently made.

It grew and grew....

By the time he became aware of the extra heat and heard the crackling it was too late.

The fire had engulfed the whole side of the boat and water was beginning to seep in.

He frantically tried to do what he could but it was to no avail. His every attempt led nowhere and it was clear that he was sinking.

Far from the safety of land and without knowing how to swim he all too soon realized his fate and not much after, succumbed to the icy waters. Now murky and reflecting the final flares of the burning craft.

The light was snuffed and only the eternal stars above were mute witnesses to the scene having just been played out below.

The very last part of the vessel to slip beneath the waves was the prow, upon which were the lovingly carved letters that indicated Her name.

Gaia.

Spirits and spooks

Spirituality, what a word! What an idea! To imagine that there is some rhyme or reason to existence and that it's all orchestrated by some higher power that actually has each and every one of the 8 billion or so human beans best interest at heart. WOW!

Now you notice I didn't say Religion. That's a whole other kettle of fish like stickers on the back of a BMW's behind.

Not that that particular religion is the only one of course, just that when you mention religion in this country everyone automatically thinks of Christianity. Unless you say 'hey there are other kinds too!' then people go 'oh JA! Moeslims!' and give a conspiritational wink to let you know exactly what the opinion of such misguidance is in their rolled eyes.

Religion is not up for discussion here so I'm cheating and skirting the issue by focussing on Spirituality.

Man is weird, but you already know that and to be fair woman is even weirder but I digress right off the bat. Mankind's weirdness is rooted in a gene that has a name that I don't remember but which makes us all carry the notion that there is a higher power at play here and that we have to behave. Or not, depending on your concept of spiritual pursuance.

Since the dawn of time, man has been doing weird stuff aimed at pleasing Gods from all walks of eternity and lopping off the heads of anything with a head or two or three or more, to appease these Gods and send rain or a bicycle whichever you decide upon. It must work obviously as rain hasn't stopped and people get bikes all the time.

I personally like the Amerindians concept of a Great Spirit that was all seeing and all-pervading and if you dropped enough peyote mixed with a healthy dollop of mescaline, you could talk or be talked to directly without any operator listening on the line or anything. It amazes me how in fact these Indians managed to figure out some weird stuff that they attributed to the guidance of said great Spirit such as planting fish..of all things! ;) Along with their corn plants to enable them to grow better. Today we know that it's the nitrogen in the fish and other things that make the mielies grow taller, stronger and have no Piscean odour or taste to speak of. But how on...Earth? Did they know that way back then? Other weirder stuffs too but you get the point.

Now you can be Spiritual and be religious but that's not what I'm trying to get at here. Spirituality to me is not quite such pie in the sky stuff as it may be for many others and here's the way I see it.

To start off by being contradictory, every day is the Sabbath! Not in the sense that you braai and drink copious amounts of beer but in the sense that no one day is more 'holy' than any other. It's selfish as hell as it's focussed entirely on cultivation of self and I offer no excuse. There is no 'charity' as in helping others. I believe in empowerment and so whatever so called 'help' I may offer someone is a by-product of the 'spiritual' path I'm on and not a practice or goal. So, to turn the regular idea of 'oh! I'm soo spiritual, because I help others in need' is not the way I see it. To help others in need or whatever is an outcome of selfish spiritual practice and not a result. Point made or should I repeat myself a third time?

What are the practices?

It can be anything. Driving your car can be a spiritual experience depending on how you approach it and that is essentially the gist of it. Your approach. Your attitude.

Your very desire to address some of your own personal weaknesses is the root of spiritual growth. To begin by soberly appraising your entire makeup and assessing strong or weak points or parts you would like to change. Basically you have a choice. If you're completely happy with who and what you are and believe that there's really nothing you can do to become a better person in some way then you are ...rare! Or deluded, or both. By deciding to become a better person you automatically begin to walk a more spiritual path.

What is a better person? This is up to you. To Hitler it may have meant one thing but you it may mean another. YOU decide! And only YOU can know if this is the 'right' choice. That's the tough part. With religion, you have guidelines and rules but with pure spirituality to have to define those for yourself and the beauty is that you can crib from everywhere! You can take a Christian principle such as don't do to the other guy what you don't want him to do to your dog and say "that's cool!' and include it in your own doctrine of sorts. Then, once that's written in stone the job is to include it in your life on a daily basis. That's the path. There is no right or wrong way and only you can know that you have strayed. Now I hear you grumbling. Bullshit! And maybe you're right, but I don't care! It's MY path and there's no pressure on you to follow or agree to it. On one condition and ONE only. Does it impinge on another's freedom as a human being? If it does then it must be flawed.

Thing is. Most people, when left to their own devises and having reached a certain level of maturity will naturally make choices that will not be in direct conflict with the freedom and right of others to be who and what they are. Choosing a more spiritual way of behaving means that you are choosing to respond rather than knee jerk react and so makes you a more aware and rational person. Practicing this day by day means that you become that. Not pretend, act or create a charade to have to constantly maintain, but rather to begin acting spontaneously in the manner that you train yourself through the initial constant awareness of self and remedial action in real time. It means you become more humble in that you realise and admit openly if only to yourself anyway, that you have flaws and you're working on it. A kind of a paradox in that you're selfish and re-creating your own world but it results in your added humility and acceptance that your life is a process and a masterpiece in the making. Constantly! And the add-on effect is that your relationships with others in general, will improve. By removing the barriers you have created by having pre conceived notions of what another person should or shouldn't be or do, you will discover that you are able to accept them a little easier and so avoid the conflicting emotions, stress and real conflict in most cases that arise from this mode of thinking.

Many people seem to think that walking a spiritual path more consciously now that they have decided to do so results in one becoming a Buddha or Jesus or holy person or if not, then at least a little closer to glowing in the dark than the next guy. This is an added delusion and fed by the ego which always reserves prime position. A lot is written about ego and I won't add to it except to say that the ego is elusive and then extrapolate below...

Where is it? What is it? Just a puff of smoke when you try to grab it but its flaw is that it always leaves a trace of some kind which gives it away. Easiest way to check the ego is to see whether it's employing some emotion to unbalance you. Another folly is to think that the ego must be eradicated completely otherwise you stand no chance to become a sage. Some spiritual paths follow this track but for my own part I feel that there is healthy and unhealthy ego. The unhealthy is simply self-serving and serves no one, including oneself, in the long run. The other approach is to put ego to good use and employ it with discretion. This discretion can only be gained through time and practice and a double edged sword that can and does cut both ways.

In the east the mind which houses the ego is depicted as a Tiger! And a rather humorous sculpture I saw in China was one of a guy bashing the tiger over the head with a large sledgehammer!! I laughed and was asked by someone not familiar with eastern thought what was so funny and explained. The person thought it was a wonderful concept and my own ego was stroked due to my impartation of such esoteric knowledge, I have to admit.

Thing was, I was wondering at the time. Who is wielding the hammer? What is the hammer? But the message that the sculptor tried to convey was clear. Smash the mind! And some eastern philosophies believe it's simple. One blow from the Zen masters stick and mind is gone and ego with it. For my part, I'm not sure how easy that is. That would mean that a spiritual path would consist of a single step! Boom! Gone! So why have priests, gurus, and disciplines? I understand the concept yet I feel it's over simplified and that just as we have built the ego and reliance on mind for years it just seems prudent that it would take a while to unlearn those modes of thinking and resultant behaviour. Gurus would tell me that it's my clinging that creates such complexity but I don't know any other way and so it's my path and my arduous effort that will achieve some results over time although I dearly wish that one bang to the head would enlighten me and unburden me from intracranial gymnastics.

That's the path. It's a one-step journey for very rare individuals but for the rest of us it's a daily grind or stroll in the park, depending on our approach.

We have mentioned some or the rewards of walking this rocky road but that's something to be forgotten. There is no destination; it's the steps, each and every one. One bite of the pizza at a time and chew a lot before swallowing to enable effective digestion and to lessen the occurrence of burps and heartburn.

The road goes up as well as down and sometimes the lack of signage will mean you go astray but the longer you walk the better your GPS becomes and before you know it, it's just another day in familiar surroundings and you can begin to relax and enjoy the trip and even perhaps stop to smell the roses along the way.

Bon voyage!

Veldschool

I grew up with a black person in my house. She was my proxy mom and carried, fed, changed my nappies and cared for me with as much love and attention as any mother would. She was a special woman as it was said that she was a "Sangoma" but whether that's really true I couldn't know. She definitely knew about herbs and treated people on occasion as well as acting as midwife to friends and strangers alike. She was also one of the elders in her church which was an African church who's congregation met each Sunday out in the veld and would sing and chant in the rock lined circle they had established in the earth. She was a kind of "in betweener" in that the traditional values and beliefs of the African people at that stage were still firmly entrenched in their minds and actions yet they also incorporated a European approach to Christianity by singing hymns and prayer and so on. So they would worship in the bush in a sort of hybridized version of organized religion. I have mentioned Andries at length who taught me so many things and particularly what it really meant to be a man in the true sense of the word.

I grew up with all this and absolutely no knowledge whatsoever that Nelson Mandela existed. The first exposure I had to his name was noticing some graffiti on an underpass where there were slogans like "Power to the people" written hastily in black spray and also "free Nelson Mandela" Someone had added underneath 'With every box of Kellogg's cornflakes!" I asked about this and was told that it was the work of "the terrorrrists" Terrorism, of course was the huge blanket of fear that we were all brought up beneath. Communism was the buzzword and as I understood it "they" were infiltrating "us" at every turn and mostly attacking our subconscious minds... If we weren't extra vigilant we would end up being nothing more than slaves to the "Blacks"

This is typical from the time that I grew up.

For me, I think, the main split happened when I decided to leave the Afrikaans school. A few experiences that I had had compacted my decision. The boy who acted as the referee to many of my fights, lived just around the corner from our house and we were quite close for a time. He was the "uber kind" and was the best academic, runner, rugby player and 2nd best swimmer in our class of course! He had convinced my mom that he would help me with my homework and so a few days each week I was allowed to skip the centre and I would go and visit Deon where, true to his word we would do homework, for 1 minute and then spend the rest of the afternoon raising hell in the neighborhood. Usually the "game" would be a test of strength or simply stupid activities to see how much punishment we could tolerate from his older brother before we lost consciousness or were decapitated or both. The thing that struck me was when we would go and have lunch at his house. He like everyone had a black domestic servant who he would call " die meit" which means "the maid" but which has a rather negative connotation much like "nigger bitch" I suppose. He was only 11 years old and he would speak to this woman with absolute contempt which shocked me as I was taught to respect my elders regardless. I was not only shocked but more confused in a way as I simply could not understand his hostility toward her and towards all the " die fokken kaffirs" But at school even the teachers would take that tone and you would hear them ranting in the staffroom at breaks how it would be a good idea to blow up the mines to take care of the lot of them and suchlike talk. Them and us. I just didn't feel so much like I was one of us so much anymore. I have never called anyone a kaffir in my life and it's a form of address that when I hear it just boils my blood. Even just relating this story my skin crawls to write it. Its such a stupid term anyway as the real meaning of the word would apply to the Christians automatically as it is an Arabic term meaning "non believer" in Allah of course. Anyway, Deon used to order her around and she would bow and scrape and then go outside and curse him in Zulu which he couldn't understand. I would and would treat her with respect which would earn his derision and on occasion she would get fed up and tell him that he could learn some manners from me and his response was to threaten her with a beating. This from an 11 year old. With total impunity. For Deon it was the right thing to do. He was merely behaving as he was taught. He didn't want to be seen as weak. I couldn't relate to it and it bothered me no end. It was a total contrast going to visit my English friend Grant. If he had spoken that way to his servant he would have received a beating from his father that he would never forget. Daisy, their housemaid was more like a friend or perhaps colleague than a "Worker" She also lived outside in her own little room and so on but she was treated with a lot more respect and I would be intensely aware of the difference between Deon and Grants home.

Perhaps reading this you may be thinking how crazy it was for practically every household having a servant but growing up with it was accepted as a part of life. You grew up saying " the garden boy" I remember one day at age 23 saying "where's the boy?" realizing at the same moment..Oh my God! I'm talking about Elvis here! Wow! Is this me? The man who works with us. A man old enough to be my father and I'm calling him "the garden boy" For Chrissakes, is it that deeply ingrained in me?

It was the kind of life that we lived. We wouldn't consider things like that and yet if someone had addressed or referred to you in that fashion you would be immediately insulted. Looking back I'm amazes at the way our realities were "conditioned" There was no freedom of the press so you would never know what was actually happening and it may be happening just down the road.

The first main event that literally rocked my boat and in fact everyone's boat was in 76 on the occasion of the "Soweto riots" The day of the event, I was in my street playing cricket with one of my neighbors when we were interrupted by the boys mom who told him to get straight inside and told me to go directly home. I asked her what all the fuss was about and she said "the blacks have gone berserk! and are on their way. Go home!" I remember standing there and said " Anyone comes near me and they will get a taste of this!" waving my bat threateningly through the air while taking a good look at the bottom of the street to make sure that it actually was safe. The fact that THOUSANDS of people were dancing in unison and creating all kinds of havoc never occurred to me. I had never seen a single picture of a demonstration, riot or any such thing and there simply wasn't anything in my mind that would come close to providing me with a conscious image to relate to. Today, with the internet and cable television news it is inconceivable but in those days it was simple cold fact. The news that we did get was of "them" burning down the schools which had been built with white tax payers money and naturally just impacted the rift between the races. The standard gripe was that 'we build their schools with our hard work and this is what they do!"

I'm in my 20's. My friend Shaun and I, the two skate punks, decide we are going to go to Vereeniging, a town some 40 or so km away as there is a skateboard park there. We decide to jump the train and go in the 3rd class compartment as there is no conductor checking these carriages.

Now we hopped the train that went through Soweto due to the fact that we had never actually seen the place from the inside and were curious.

We enter the place shortly after leaving JHB station and the first impression was of row upon row upon row of small houses which were aptly named "matchboxes" I had seen such images before in paintings by the more politically orientated artists that would depict these images and I truly thought that it was exaggerated to produce a dramatic effect. I was amazed to discover that the artists never could have captured the immensity if they tried.

We enter and I expect that soon we will be out into the country and on our way. It takes three hours for us to get through this endless expense of "matchboxes" Its not a pleasant trip. At the stations, there are young kids who run beside the train and hop on clutching desperately and beg through the tiny open slit of a window. When they see us in "their" train they go ballistic and hurl abuse, spit and try to throw rocks through the small window. Eventually one of the many package laden ladies comes to us and suggests that we sit on the floor and in so doing will not attract so much attention and be safer. We hastily take her advice and although the trip is not as intense it is still pretty hairy as when the kids see us, they uniformly take an aggressive attitude.

I am shaken to my boots. Not by fear but by the enormity of the place. Hill after hill of these small houses. At one stage I suspect we are traveling in circles but its not that simple. The black adults on the train are quiet and more than a little uncomfortable with us being there and more than one moves to another carriage at first opportunity. I am always amazed how some people will risk so much to help us as reprisals are swift and brutal for so called "collaborators' Taken to its extreme in the horrific images of people being "necklaced" by having a tire placed around there necks and filled with petrol and being set alight. More than one lady was friendly and helpful.

We eventually get to Vereeniging, a dismal enclave of right wing, ultra nationalist thinking and walk no more than 20m from the station before we are pulled over by the police and roughly searched and pushed around when nothing is found.

We go and skate and decide not to stay overnight as planned and hitchhike back to JHB the same day. We were both deeply moved and disturbed by the experience and the fact that we were stopped by the police so soon after our experience made me feel how very out of place we were.

It is the only time I have ever been "into" Soweto.

Consider that my house was located almost exactly 15 km from the beginning of Soweto. It was a straight drive on the freeway and one that my dad and I often did when we went to ride our motorbikes in the veld in the vicinity of the township. Soweto stands for South Western Township by the way. I had never been there. I hadn't even seen it from a distance.

My dad used to take his point 22 revolver with him "just in case" I was never sure of what. Snakes I thought. I never considered how in hell you were supposed to draw, aim and shoot a snake while you were screaming along a dirt track at a death defying speed or for that matter, what danger a snake would pose in such a situation.

My dad, being basically an immigrant and completely immersed in his cars and bikes, took no interest in politics whatsoever and for the most part could be considered apolitical. I don't think he was legible to vote in any case. He became a South African citizen at the age of 83! And only because he thought he could wangle some pension money!

The 76 riots were a turning point for many people as regards their awareness of the unique situation that we were faced with in South Africa. For me it was undoubtedly a major event. I would return from a vacation in Mozambique and the conversation at school would be centered around the black white situation.

Although my knowledge of South African history was fairly comprehensive and I could tell you all about battles and heroes, I simply would not have been able to tell you very much at all about anything beyond the time that the Republic was established. My exposure to sculpture consisted of seeing a bass relief on the library wall of a bunch of oxen and wagons and guys with floppy hats riding horses. All from a much earlier time. There wasn't much from the 50's for example. To me the 50's were a time when roadhouses became popular and Chevy's and greasy haired guys with boxes of smokes rolled up in the sleeves of white t shirts.

In my home we practically never discussed politics. It wasn't a conscious thing, it just didn't seem relevant with all the activity in our various lives the conversation would centre around day to day events. My folks were not what I would call politically oriented like some other peoples parents were. I would probably say that they could be classified as "rationalists" if there is such a thing. My dad's attitude was that black people were simply a little primitive and were so due to the fact that the

British Empire was a little slow in colonizing the place. Blacks went bad per se, just a little ignorant and needed to be educated to catch up to the Europeans much in the same way that the British had done in India. He never felt hatred or animosity of any kind and treated everyone with dignity and respect. My mom was conservative and based her opinions more in line with those of Christian charity than of right wing politics. My folks were quite typical and a world away from the archetypal image that has been propagated by the international press of every white person being a Nazi and every black a slave. That's basically a load of horse and I'll fight anyone who wants to argue with me about that.

Apartheid was something that I didn't even begin to understand and one of the first questions I asked Aya at the age of about 14 was, "well, you're black and I am white, what do *you* think of this Apartheid?' It needs to be stated that I didn't even know that Apartheid was a law. I didn't know it was the name for these collection of laws. I had just heard the word and knew that it referred to the separation of blacks and whites. The fact that they and we would have separate public amenities such as busses and toilets and even park benches. There was a toilet for 'Whites" and one for "Non Whites" You would never go into the non whites one since it always stank and didn't have seats or paper and you could get raped so it was out of bounds. Aya was reticent, to understate, and said we shouldn't really talk about it since it leads nowhere but I was persistent and eventually one day while I was helping her in the kitchen she relented and turned to me and said' If you have a cow, and it's black and white and you want the cow to be black. So you take your knife and you cut out the white pieces. What have you got?" ..."and if you have the same cow and you want it to be white and you cut out all the black pieces,..What have you got? Hmm?" I thought about this and wasn't sure what to say and she turned to me and looked me straight in the eye and said ' You have a dead cow!" she turned and continued with her work laughing and shaking her head the way she would do so often. That is the only time and the only thing ever, that Aya said something pertaining to the political situation. She was a devout and God fearing woman and considered everything below the Almighty a waste of time to sit around talking about.

My first exposure to political thought in a formal setting was when I was 15 years old. It happened at Veldschool. Literally- Field school. The very name conjures up images of bubbling streams and huntin' and fishin' straight out of National Geographic. I thought we would learn to identify edible plants and track wild beasts and identify each and every star in the southern sky...but sadly... I was mistaken.

Veldschool turned out to be nothing less than an intensive week of indoctrination and basically preparation for our soon to be undertaken National Service. As I had changed schools during this period I had the dubious honor of attending Veldschool twice. Both times at the same location.

The first time I went there, there was the main master who dressed in khaki safari suit complete with hat and a leopard skin band. I swear! He would rant and rave and have us marching up and down the square and leopard crawling through the dirt and thorns at 5am. He pissed everyone off. One morning it was particularly rough and a little later in the day he was supposed to deliver a lecture. All the boys were sitting sullenly waiting for the fool and as he strutted up, one of the boys said "here comes Hitler!" He heard it and screamed" WHO SAID THAT?!! HA?!!" Nobody as much as squeaked. He said something to the effect of " somebody got something to say? HA!? Cummon speak up. NOW's the time" I thought to myself.."better get your hand up quick" and so up it shot. It was the only one... to the accompanying groan of the rest of the boys..

So I put it to him like this in a very calm and respectful way." Sir your attitude works with the Afrikaans school as that is what they understand but we are used to debate and don't respond very well to being ordered around. We are quite capable of superseding their achievements but we need to do it as a team and basically if you changed your attitude somewhat we will prove it to you. So yes, the boys think of you as a Hitler as that is the way that you present yourself to us" and I sat down. Everyone was speechless and I was ready to pee in my pants. The funny thing was that only ONE boy stood up and supported me when he asked the boys if they agreed. All the tough big mouthed bully boys were as quiet as churchmouses. Ill never learn.

It was late afternoon at the camp. We were all billeted in tents and slept on metal bunks. The boys were divided into "groups" and there was stiff competition between the better ones who took the whole thing very seriously.

As is quite usual at this time of year, late afternoon thunderstorms were commonplace and brutal. One was brewing and the boys scurried around trying to retrieve as many important things they could and deposit them in the dubious security of the tent. I, being the group leader and well aware of how hopelessly outclassed my merry band of bandits were when compared with the main group of "Jocks" who beat us hands down at everything, decided to use the elements to our advantage and take this golden opportunity to strike like lightning and loosen the guy ropes on their tent!

The result was awesome! The storm blew in with stroboscopic lightning and thunder and just before the wind and hail pelted down , the gale force wind billowed out the tent like a hot air balloon and launched it clear, to eventually come to rest about 1 km away!

The physically fit "Jock" team ran physically after it and finally after much dragging and wrestling, managed to re pitch said tent after the storm had abated and completely soaked all their belongings to the bone.

They spent the rest of the week squelching round in the mud pool <u>inside</u> their tent!

It was magnificent!

A few weeks later, after I had changed schools it was our turn to go to Veldschool and as fate would have it we went to the same one!. Out of a whole country with a whole network of them we had to go there!. As I got off the bus he was there like a drill sergeant and recognizing me he exclaimed " welcome back comrade" and kicked me so hard up the backside that I honestly thought he had fractured the bones in my coccyx. Bastard.

The reason he had addressed me in that way was due to a lecture that we had been given by the headmaster of the Veldschool on the previous occasion.

It was entitled. "Communism"

The headmaster was a shortish, powerfully built man who was feared by the rest of his staff. He gave a few talks and was intolerant of any kinds of "nonsense" his punishment exercises were killing and he didn't accept anything less than the parameters he had set. If you had to run around the square in 30 seconds. 31 was unacceptable and there was no quitting until the target was reached even if you were still there crawling around the following day. It had to be done. He gave a very basic overview of the communist system and when he got to the part where, as he put it " the 10th phase is when the government dissolves and the country is ruled by the people" My hand shot up and I said " wow! That sounds like a bloody good idea Sir!" He went ballistic, accompanied by the knee jerk comments from the other boys, vigorously voicing their indignation and doing the expected thing. " Ooh! Aahh!" He went on about the atrocities committed by Stalin and the lecture went way beyond the allocated time. At the end he asked me if I still thought the same and I stood up and said "Yes Sir, I do" It brought the house down.

That evening I was summoned to his quarters and was expecting to be caned but it turned out that we had the most intensely illuminating conversation ever. He informed me that what he was about to say was between us and not for the boys to hear about and proceeded to tell me about his activities as an agent in Russia and some of the crazy things he had experienced. He was way smart and better read than anyone I had ever met and at the close of the evening he confided to me that he also thought "it was a bloody good idea" But sternly reprimanded me and said that it would be far better if I didn't voice my opinion so openly. The comical end to the evening was that he said. "well everyone is expecting that I punish you so play the game OK?" he then took out a cane and proceeded to raise his voice and shout abuse and then whacked the note book on his desk loudly and shouted " NOW GET OUT OF MY SIGHT!" I wasn't sure whether to laugh or cry as, when he took out the cane I was sure he was going to tan my hide and upon seeing the show was both shocked and relieved. When I got back to the tent the boys asked what happened and I just said " I don't want to talk about it" The next morning, Hitler himself stood grinning at me with a look that said clearly "see what happens to Kaffir boeties like you HA!" I Looked away and continued "to play the game" as I had promised.

This is the first time I have ever related that story to anyone. It was an experience that was pivotal. It served to confuse me more than anything as the clear definition between the "goodies" and the "baddies" was beginning to blur and it would be years before I would realize how much of a risk the man took in confiding in me.

It was common for the naughty boys to smoke and on Veldschool it was also a common thing to see how much hell you could raise and get away with. The naughty boys in my vicinity decided that it was time to "Get High!" And so all the stories came out but no material with which to get high on. No it was a common story that if one would be so inclined, one could smoke "Cowshit!" and be guaranteed of an amazing 'Buzz" So off we go to acquire some dryish cow manure of which there is an abundance in the area. True to form we all have a puff and settle back for the promised "Trip" and of course. Nothing!!

Except a crap taste in my mouth!!

Hitler pretty much kept his distance from me throughout the week. I refrained from provoking him which he must have thought was due to "the lesson" that I had been given by the headmaster but on the last day, as we were boarding the bus. I spotted him and walked over and told him exactly what I thought of a man who likes to kick someone from behind without provocation or warning. In fluent Afrikaans!!

He just gaped at me as I walked away.

Other "talks" we were treated to dealt with subjects such as the subliminal war being waged and enlightened us to the REAL meaning behind wearing jeans for one. Buying records by the pop group ABBA was giving funds directly to the enemy to buy arms. Jeans were a secret sign of membership in the banned communist party. The peace sign was actually a secret Satanist symbol as it depicted a cross with the horizontal pieces broken and leaning on the upright. Soweto was an anagram for what I don't remember..and so on and so forth....

Subsequently I would be a lot more aware of what was going on around me. I would listen to political conversations by the other students and do my best to remain rational and try to understand this system that I thought qualified as one of the dumbest ideas ever conceived by a head of state.

The absolute use of force and Gestapo tactics..how long did they think it could last? It's beyond me. Still.

I know that the way I have portrayed things so far is to kind of cover the Afrikaaners with the racist blanket and cover the English with the liberal one but things are never so simple.

South Africa was not simply comprised of Blacks and Whites. It is a vast tapestry of cultures, backgrounds, religions and attitudes that cannot simply be divided in the typical pie graph, geography class manner. It comes as a shock to me that even today in a world that knows the internet and cable television that I encounter educated adults that take the view that South Africa is White and Black. I teach English online and my first question to students that give me this picture is "which blacks?' Invariably I am faced with incomprehension. People have no idea of what I am asking. My response is to give a short lecture outlining in the broadest terms the societal framework. I'm going to do that here but must insert as a disclaimer that it is very, very simplistic and based on my own subjective view and should be taken as such.

Whites come in two general flavors. English and Afrikaans. The English dudes (and dudesses) come from England! And for the most part controlled business and private sector activities. They would be liberal in terms of political orientation. Except for the ones who were not. The Afrikaans dudes and their spouses come from Holland and France and their dogs from Germany. They were, by and large right wing and lived in government houses because they were Policemen, Firemen or worked in the post office. Afrikaners played Rugby and Englishmen played also Rugby but knew how to play Football too. It was called Soccer. Both drank lots of beer.

The Jews were English and controlled all the money. They were the Doctors, Dentists, Orthodontists, Lawyers, Bankers and Rabbis. South Africa's Jewish population was large and so were their houses. They drank both beer and wine and preferred golf and tennis. They didn't mind if other people played Rugby or Football.

Now for the Blacks...There are a lot of them and they come from South Africa but not all from the same place. I don't know all of them but the two largest groups are the Zulus, a proud and fierce warrior nation and the Xhosa who have a name that can only be pronounced by South Africans who have put in the sufficient hours of practice and don't chew gum and talk simultaneously. They are by contrast, a fierce and proud warrior nation. Both are ruled by a king...I think, but they live on opposite sides of the same river. There are a number of other nations too. Notice I don't say tribes as they are much smaller and don't make the cut. There are many tribes too but I wont get into it. Sotho's both north and south, Swazis who live in Swaziland! But travel frequently, Shangaan, Griquas, Bushmen or San people, Tswana, and a whole array of others I just don't remember at this point or have omitted due to lack of certainty of national status. The fact remains that there are a lot of them and what's interesting is that they are all distinctly distinct from one another in terms of language, mythology, tribal law, social customs and so on. Men worked in the mines and women in the houses. They all like football and drink lots of beer. They are not all friendly with each other though and some are traditionally enemies and hate each others guts.

But love each others women.

That would be very simple if the proverbial pie would stop there.

But what about the Coloureds? Coloureds you ask...Well yes. During Apartheid there was the clear distinction between the rights of whites and lack of rights for blacks but what about If you were an Indian? Chinese? Malayan? Egyptian? Where did the law provide for you?

Good question!

These guys are easy deal with as they have clearly defined cultural and national identities but the "coloureds" are a different story. They are people who are the result of interbreeding between the early mariners and settlers in the country and the slaves that they either were transporting or had brought with them to do all the hard work. Many people from Malaysia who are predominantly Moslems. Indians would be lumped into this category along with all the other nationalities mentioned that were unfortunate enough to have a less than milky complexion. Here we find the merchants. Greek and Portuguese were traditionally the café owners and greengrocers. Italians the restaurateurs. Indians owned haberdasheries and curry houses. These guys preferred drinking wine and cricket was sport of choice except for the Portuguese and Italians who drank wine but loved football, didn't understand rugby and hated cricket.

The political orientation for the last two groups is not of any consequence as the majority couldn't vote anyway.

They sleep under the wide and ill defined blanket known as. The grey areas..

So there it is, The South African socio political structure in a nutshell.

Simple.

The green is grasser

Green!..perhaps you have heard of it.

Well...How green? There's dark green, light green, bright green and I suppose a paler shade of green too.

What does it all mean?

Sustainability, recycling, bio fuel, garbage separation...the list goes on and on. Is it anything more than just a new way to sell stuff? Like sex! Its a good way to get your product out there and lets face it. Green is cool! And getting cooler by the minute. When I was in Israel I was reminded of how cool it is by the new "green buses" that are run by the Egged company. Basically the advert on TV said that the whole scene was "going green" what this meant in reality is that the buses got a brand new coat of paint and underwent a whole new ad campaign that cost a whole lot of the green stuff we are all quite attached to.

Thats the green stuff at the crux of the matter. When being green shows a profit then it will all pan out. Until then ....well....NADA!

Now the question needs to be asked..Why go green in the first place? Well...Um...to save the planet!! Yeah! Be green and it will all just be so cool here on Earth.. Actually its going to be HOT! From what I'm told anyhow.

I'm currently in New Zealand and its a pretty green place. You have recycling centers and the guys wont let you drop anchor if you have been dropping bombs out there in the ocean, also you aren't welcome if you have been hunting whales. Thats a kind of a good thing by my reckoning but I am confused as to what it means in the so called bigger picture. Does all this Eco warriorship actually result in a multicolored rainbow for all in the end??

Who knows?

I go to the supermarket and buy my veggies and have to practically stage a one man protest when I get to the checkout counter and refuse the plastic bags that I am inundated with. A bag for the veggies (each different type) goes into another bag and then into my backpack. I am referred to as "the nutter" as I refuse ANY bags and plonk it all into my backpack before getting on my re cycled bike and heading off home. When I ask for a bag, as I have none to put my garbage in I am reluctantly given ONE! And with the look of pure disgust that goes with the service.

I don't get it.

I worked at an alternative type building when I first got here and was well impressed with the owners use of "sell by" products that he got from the local supermarket. Now get this...He would get the produce delivered to his doorstep as "pig food" as it was more economically viable for the company to drop it off than to get the garbage guys to take it away. The guy who owned the house was also a Christian and so distributed the "good" stuff to members of the community who were impoverished and so in need of these things. The catch was that the company delivering the food for the pigs were and are not to know that the food was being distributed to PEOPLE!!! Why? Because it wasn't profitable!! So they could actually deliver food for pigs on condition that it wasn't used to feed people in need.

Go figure...

Lots of figuring to be done though. If you figure out the amount of space and feasibility it would take to feed the inhabitants of earth on vegetables the facts are less than encouraging. There simply isn't enough space and arable land to sustain the population as a group of vegetarians. Sad but true. Also true is the fact that according to the "experts" we have already passed the threshold of irreversible climate change. According to some it would take another 1000 years to reach a point where our current catastrophe would be brought back into order. According to others we have passed that point and are well on the way to oblivion.

Al Gore made a pretty good flick/doccie about how much shit we are really in and in so doing got the Nobel prize for peace. Well done dude!! What we haven't seen just yet are the things we can do to avert impending disaster. Put a gray water system into your garden? Plant out your own veggies, etc...all good ideas but how effective in practice? Not to mention the labor intensivity of the whole thing. It's HARD work to make your own garden and you need to devote time and correct practice to keep the thing afloat and in the reasonable parameters of what is actually realistic in terms of yield. It's clearly not for everyone or anyone who has a job and family and the vestiges of a standard..life

So far the grass is looking a bit dismal...even dismaler is the average attitude of Mr Joseph Public. How do you convince this dude to give up the weekend barbie??? Some things are just not to be messed with and come hell or high water or both it just wont do to tell someone that by eating lamb chops you are contributing to the depletion of the atmosphere.. How so you may ask?...Well it simple.. Sheep fart!! In New Zealand alone there are only 35 million sheep. It used to be double but now due to cattle prices being better than sheep there are only half. Cattle are 35 million too so you're back to the magical number of 70 million odd head of livestock. Heres the kicker!...Cows fart too... So.. 70 million

farts per day add up to an enormous amount of Methane being released into the atmosphere and methane is a gas that is 24 times more damaging to the sky than co2 that you fart out every time you rev your motor at the traffic lights. So here you are revving your motor on the way to the barbie....

So....whats to be done?? Well I try as an individual based on the maxim that one person multiplied equals...etc. But is it really significant? I like to shower. Yup! Its true and I probably use more water in one session than Ethiopia drinks in 6 months. So what? I live in an area that receives 9 meters a year of rain and there's no shortage. The fuel I burn heating my water is provided by the hydroelectric scheme that is fueled by..water from rainfall mainly. If I had to bottle all my save d water from reduced showers and sent it to the Sahara, would it help? Its a bit like being chastised for not eating you beans due to the starving millions in Africa.....

I see people moving to "Eco villages" which are almost completely self sustainable with the nearly zero footprint and so on and the inhabitants number in the hundreds. Compared with an average city of gas guzzling, water drinking, methane farting humans how well does it compare? City's are gunk spewing monsters and it will take AGES to try to change the current trend. They are going to continue for a long time..or will they?

There is light at the end of the tunnel though. A speck to be sure but some light nevertheless. In Brazil one city took the bull by the balls and started implementing change and converted and average, drab city into a veritable tourist attraction. How? Well they started out by changing the main road through the cbd!! In this way they re vamped the whole way in which people commuted through the city and in doing so reduced carbon emissions significantly. The story just goes uphill from there. It's a modern marvel and shows what people can accomplish when change is instituted at the administrative level. Its a long and beautiful story that I wont explore but an inspiration nevertheless. Not so as regards our modern world empire, otherwise known as The United Mistakes Of America.

Here, stories of ecologically responsible communities is a little less inspiring. There are so many wonderful and innovative people who have had the gift of growing up in the states and have produced revolutionary ways to retro fit existing neighborhoods and make them more efficient and are plagued by red tape and by laws that strangle their ability to create more than one project that works. There are projects that have completely revolutionized the average suburbian jungle and transformed it into a working and wonderfully humane area to live and work in and yet due to bullshit basically have not been able to be duplicated. This resulted in the obvious disillusionment of the protagonists in the various projects. I know I'm being vague but these are real, very real and soul destroying events that are easily researched and verified. Such as the electric car that was a Godsend and was somehow, for some reason, blown clean out of the water despite public protest. A sad, sad story indeed. You can Google "The death of the electric car" if you still think I'm more full of shit than I really am.

So? Where will change be instituted? The simple answer is " the youth" but sadly it seems that there isn't enough time left for a 20 year educational plan to be set in place and duly implemented.

So I'm left in practically the same position as before except that I now know how deep the shit is and still haven't the faintest clue as to where to swim to or why.

Will cockroaches inherit the Earth? I really don't know and if I have any say over the matter I say. "Spray the bastards!!" as I and my kind are the rulers of this planet and its not something I plan to give up just yet.

I love this Earth and almost everything in it and I'm a naïve, idealistic, stupid, green,aging Punk rocker and I'm going to do my damnedests to ensure that this Earth stays in the hands of those that have been given custodianship and have the power to save or destroy this amazing planet that we all call home.

Whatever the cost.

So there!!

Where does that leave us?.................. Good question.......... if I may say so myself.

Aftermaththematics

Hindsight is 20/20 or so they say....

I guess you would have to be facing backwards in order to see that well.

Who cares how well you see anyway! What difference does it make if you can see something in hard focus? Can you perceive something in hard focus? Is your perception well developed enough to make the quantum leap into understanding? Is your focus centered on the wrong spot? Can you direct your focus into the aspects that need to be focused on in order to reach a full comprehensive picture that could be considered objective?

Facts are hard focus and intuitive cognition is like looking through a frosted glass window in the rain.

Both cranial vistas are valid as they possess a certain element of so called truth. The difference of course is each party's subjective observances. Conflict arises when any party insists on their perception as being more valid or conversely the others invalidity and attempts to enforce this view upon the other.

Power is the ability to control whichever point of view that is dominant and maintain the differential.

Justice is a concept that is confusing as it attempts to balance activities of the past with preordained, controlled activities of the future.

Hindsight is the analytical tool that enables you to learn. Hindsight is the faculty that never sleeps. Hindsight should be viewed as a continuum with projection on its opposite pole and not as a dualistic entity.

The vehicle of mind spends most of its time cruising back and forth along this highway and leaves little room for conscious awareness of the here, now existence.

Minds on the motorway are busy minds. Trying to overtake. Changing direction. Busy.

Minds in the here now are tranquil. The clutch is always ready to engaged and not affected by the acceleration or braking of the emotions. Minds in the here now move without effort.

Analytical retrospection allows you to move forward with a clearer vision of where it is you would like to go.

Winston Churchill, that iconic testament to clean living and good health once said something to the effect that one's ability to see into the future is directly proportional to the depth one is able to look back into the past. I would agree, but add that it is dependent on one's ability to adapt to any given new situation with that knowledge in mind.

So what's the point?

Well in my case it is trying to simply not make the same mistake twice and I am a repeat offender when it comes to this.

I screw up on a regular basis. I am a chronic screwer upper and sick and tired of being sick and tired of messing up my precarious existence with impulsive and often irresponsible actions. I am in effect a victim of myself and have had enough of my self-inflicted misery.

How to change? A leopard cannot change its spots and an old dog couldn't be bothered with all that effort required to learn a new trick.

Yet a more comfortable and productive future may be in store if this crusty old mutt only would. As it is I have a distinct preference for stripes and perhaps this is the root of my continual downfall. The world wants spotty leopards and won't tolerate the linearly decorated ones.

The trick may be in recognizing the cycles if there are any and isolate the patterns that lead to the downward spiral from comfort to crisis. More than that. It is a continual effort in real time to nip the process in the bud and apply the alternative remedial mode of behavior.

It's no easy task. Note I didn't use the word impossible as I don't believe anything is impossible. It's just that sometimes it seems that way.

I also don't adhere to the notion of living life in the rear view mirror or dwelling on the glitches that make for a bumpier ride. I am more focused on eradicating faulty habits and reprogramming my obsolete hardware with a newer and updated version and ...Implementing it.

It all takes time and effort but it's a necessary expense and well worth it in the long run.

Ever noticed how some people just shine? I am especially impressed by individuals who rise above a major crisis such as suffering a physical mishap and ending up in a wheelchair or something and simply don't lie down and die. On the contrary. Somehow and in some miraculous way these people find it in themselves to accept the cards they have been dealt and rise above. It inspires awe.

Sometimes a crisis is exactly what one requires to receive a swift kick up the butt and simply get on with it.

When I was a boy, my mother took me to a home for kids with mental difficulties with the view of making me realize how fortunate I was. This was a success in part but when I think about it I am filled with a sense of pity rather than gratitude. Perhaps it would have been more effective to take me to a place where people were who were recovering or had recovered from an accident or whatever and sat me down with some of them and try to comprehend where or how it is that they managed to reach so deep and access an inner strength that I would imagine is hard wired within each of us.

I think it would have hit closer to home as we all are so fallible and..well..Shit happens.

I am on a mission. I would like to be able to play a part in having people realize the inherent talent that I firmly believe everyone possesses. First though, I feel I should be able to do so myself and thus be able to practice whatever it is that I propose to preach.

Everyone has some hidden or buried talent. Be it cooking, sewing, whatever. Usually it some kind of creative thing and if pursued would substantially enrich that person's life and in so doing give a sense of wellbeing or boosted self-esteem. In my case it is an added sense of achievement that is personal and not necessarily something that is on the list of criteria when it comes to socially accepted norms connected with what exactly success is.

Inner growth takes many forms and so it is imperative to be able to look back and see what your path has been and to be able to improvise new patterns of behavior that would lead you away from the dead end alleyways of the past and put you squarely back on track in the direction of your intended future destination.

Potential foresight may be related to hindsight but it's not always 20/20.

Myopia

I often asked my students questions like…"what would you do if you won 70 million dollars?" or " what would you do if you were the president of the world?" I ask them to try and get the conversational ball rolling and illicit opinions from them so that they forget about speaking English without mistakes and just …well…speak!

I thought it only fair to ask myself the question a few times too, and so I did!

So..what would I do with the 70 million? Well , first off I wouldn't tell you! Or anyone else either! And second…its a secret!.

As to question two I would say that if I was the President of the world I would of course declare the whole week a public holiday and make it law to eat pizza in some way or form once a week. I would then set up the Pizza Police and in so doing provide at least a few hoodlums with meaningful work in this current downtrodden economic climatic condition.

The next thing I would do is completely BAN the WWW. No! …not the Internet you fools! The damn stupid Wrestling thingey! You know, the big brutish oiled down fellows with the bleached white hair and slinky speed-o costumes that like to jump on each other! Yup! Those guys.

I would ban them outright.

Anyone even suspected of harboring sentiments would be severely punished. The whole thing is just completely out of this world. I can understand Boxing…Really! I can…well to a larger degree. The WWW is just BAD! A whole industry based on glorifying the Bully! I don't get it and get it even less when the fan base is older than 10 years of lack of age. Not to mention brain matter. Its perverse, the way in which the posturing has become the thing and bad mouthing the opponent is its own kind of event. To me it's just pandering to the lowest levels of our collective animal unconsciousness.

There are worse things though. Like WAR! War sucks big time, no matter which way you try to look at it and the funny thing is that we have not yet managed to figure out a way to disagree amongst ourselves without killing the other guy to prove were right. Thing about war is that you have to have a reason to rally up your troops. Its a small wonder that armies get any support at all as most people are so complacent they couldn't be bothered with all that shouting and marching up and down the square to gain the necessary skills to blow the enemy to kingdom come...but wait,......isn't that exactly the most popular of all rallying points? Blow the other dude into HIS/HER kingdom come and don't get blown there yourself....in a matter of speaking..

Now as I understand it so far...the baddies (according to US)..(yes its a pun!) are the guys who we try to blow into THEIR kingdom so that THEY can get the contractually contracted deal of 72 virgins in the harem, automatic one way tickets to paradise for the family but no guaranteed harem, martyr status and and unprecedented season ticket to be in contact with God himself and of course your own little palace on the grounds to enable you to be carried to and fro by your army of servants...as well as a few other juicy perks..

Now for the goodies...That's US! We by contrast get to die fighting the just fight and as soldiers in Gods righteous army you get to be pardoned for the sin of Murder and whats more get to go to heaven on condition that the rest of your life was lived righteously. No harem I'm afraid as thats a barbaric and unclean concept which plays no part in the deal unless you are a politician but then it is hush hush and no one knows the true details anyway.

So its pretty clear..they are the baddies and we are the goodies and so we will win cos Gods on our side and they believe the same thing but they're obviously wrong.

Now there is another activity that us humans are actively engaged in but mostly as participants and that is SPORT!! OOOhh the very word makes my mouth water and causes my heart to beat somewhat faster and so does the majority of the population when the word is spoken out loud.

Now there is an interesting similarity between war and sports of most kinds..especially the fighting arts. There is also a striking similarity between sport and religion in many ways although the main difference is of course the levels of attendance at the various events. Sport wins hands down. For some reason I cannot quite understand. Perhaps its the fact that religion in its own magical way is a form of war?

Anyway.... The point is that sport has become the number one method mass myopic induction and has upped religion and war in the charts. Its strange though as it seems that this interesting triangle is two sided...on the one hand you have religion and sport..a healthy marriage here. You see the participants of the international game singing their countries song and saying prayers in the locker room. You see players crossing themselves before going on the pitch and when they score goals .. in some cases anyway. Sometimes the team even has a Priest to say the prayers for the team so that God will more easily hear the prayers and thus grant the more devout team the much needed victory. So thats all Kosher.

Now duo number two.. Religion and war. Here the relationship is more complex but still an healthy friendship. Each unit has an overseeing Chaplain and he too offers prayers for his "team" to vanquish the enemy and crack lots of skulls. As does his counterpart on the other side which leads me to think that God flips a coin to decide on the winner so that he can waste no more time and get back to watching the game..

Now..War and Sport? Are they compatible? In my opinion they could be. If territorial disputes could be solved by a game of paint ball it would be really cool. First off no one would get too seriously injured. Secondly you could televise the whole event across the globe and in so doing stimulate the economy by selling advertising space and providing jobs for the officials. Not to mention the fact that a do of that kind would probably be cheaper to run than Afghanistan or Iran. The current military budget could be decimated and all that cash could go towards providing education, relief to impoverished regions, health care, and a list as long as my arm of things that would be more beneficial to the human race as a whole. You could have tactical assault courses in the Olympics and in so doing you would still provide mans baser instincts with all the excitement of a real battle but minus the bloodshed. Teams could cheer, hot dogs could be consumed and whole trends in fashion could be stimulated by the simple activity of getting two teams together and shooting the shit out of each other. Professional leagues could be established and players could be bought and sold for Gazillionz and due to the lack of wholesale slaughter on the battlefield there would be a rapidly growing population to support the whole thing.

So I would say...yes!

They are kinda compatible.

That leaves religion which as we have shown is quite happy on the Splatball Pitch.

Now to conclude...ahem!

I think its safe to state publicly that Sport is a feasible substitute for War, if only on a provisional basis.

The critical factor of course is to convince the current propagators of chaos that it is in fact in everyones interest to make the swap. If the protagonists can be made to see the value of actually laying down arms..well not even so...simply swapping ammo and making a few minor amendments to the various martyr contracts to include the triflingly little details such as actually living out a healthy life instead of having to die and to successfully defeat your opponent instead of beheading him, then perhaps there is some hope for this war thing to evolve into the higher incarnation that it can so easily and desperately needs to become.

A true sport!

It could be accomplished if it were marketed properly and if the outcomes of the games would not lead to outright war!

One of the most popular sports in the world is drinking! And usually this can be done whilst engaged in watching any sport. The danger here is that things can actually get out of hand. It has been noted and duly documented that people have actually been known to spill their drinks and even on rare occasions drop their glasses at critical moments of a particularly exciting game.

I'm sure you must have heard of Football! The English version with the round ball that is. Now, all over the world there are hardcore supporters who pledge loyalty and allegiance to the flag of their particular team and will defend to the death their geographic boundaries that demarcate the various teams juristrictive areas. It is a matter of pride to pass on from generation to generation the inbred hatred that the true supporter feels for rival teams. These rare individuals have actually managed to incorporate war into the wider circle of off pitch activities such as drinking and card collecting.

In countries such as South Africa where I had the distinct privilege of visiting once, I noticed that at a busy bank in one of the cities, a cabinet minister went unnoticed by the large group of people but a few moments later the place was brought to a standstill by the appearance of one of the Springbok Rugby players. EVERYONE was agape. (that too is a pun..albeit more subtle!) It is common for participants of most popular sports to be treated with the utmost of respect that borders on worship for some of the more dedicated fans. If it were back in the ancient Greek or Roman times these people would be immortalized in sculptures and if they were from the ancient Far East they could very likely be raised to the level of Demigod complete with temple and deity.

Sports personalities are better known than soldiers or even priests..except maybe the Pope but even he is a football fan.

It is a human condition to be more interested in the sports pages than in the current state of the game in Iran or wherever and religious things don't even make it to the paper. I mean, when last did you read the Church goers column?? Sport is constantly changing, its interesting to read about who bowled out who and in which minute. Its exciting to watch the FA Cup final or a Rugby test. Its a way of life and a point to converse with your fellow man about whilst enjoying a nice cold (or room temperature) pint at your local. Its a way to make you feel like you are a part of some greater design and worthwhile as an inhabitant of this planet. More importantly, sport is the coolest way to make you feel patriotic. A way to let you feel like you belong to something and not just anything either, something special and superior. Even for the losers there is a sense of having given your best and learning from your defeat to be stronger and rise again on another day to taste the sweet taste of VICTORY!! Sport is the way in which you are kept glued to your seat watching as a true patriot and making the country proud and your team stronger due to your avid support. Sport is all these things and more. Its a glorious thing actually as it allows you to be docile and contained within your house and safe from harm. Sport is a comfort in these troubled times when players can be bought and sold for amounts of cash that could feed Bangladesh for 62 years and on more than simple curry! When you really need to relax there is no better way than to have your blood pressure go through the roof repeatedly while you watch the agonizing moments of the end of a close match and at the end, whether winner or loser it was well worth the effort. Its an excellent way to focus the whole populations attention at the same time and make us all, good law abiding citizens in the state of Myopia.

Thats why I love sport!

Farmer Green

I know shit about farming.

But since I have been on a farm, ...boy!...... Have I learned a lot about shit!

I can spot a slop at 40m in the pouring rain whilst sliding sideways though the mud on my trusty steed and tell immediately whether its healthy or is infested with Carpuria or Ostatagia worm. I'll shout to the farmer who is zipping along on his quadricycle and shout "hey! Theres Ostatagia here!" He will come screeching to a halt. Well... as screechingly as he is able in the messy mire and ask "are you sure?' I will confidently answer him "oh yes! You can tell by the slightly deeper olive tone and of course if you pay special attention to the odor you will detect a slightly more sweet note right at the end there. It cant therefore be Carpuria!'

He would nod his a scent and inform me that we will have to re drench the entire mob.

Excuse the jargon here but farmspeak is liberally peppered with it and although it resembles English I hadn't a clue what he was on about when I first arrived here green as a greenie could be.

The first time I met said farmer was at a beach bash, where a bunch of them..old timers..were having and to which I was invited to. We got chatting and the topic of conversation drifted to why I was turning down repeated offers of pork, lamb, bull,cow and any other kinds of chops that were offered with the usual hospitality that only Kiwis are able to do with such aplomb. I confessed that although I am a South African All Black supporter I am in fact also and quite incongruently ..a vegetarian! This of course set the course of the conversation. The usual questions as to what in fact was wrong with me and then a more insightful person offered some fish to comply with said Kiwi hospitality. Upon informing them that I also did no longer partake of fish the ensuing silence and uncomprehending stares into space was broken by a kind soul breaking into song with his beat up guitar and all used the diversion to sing along with gusto.

It was not much later that the farmer sidled up to me and with a slightly quizzical expression confessed that he had never actually spoken to a vegetarian! We continued to converse whilst guzzling down our respective beverages and it was so that I ended up a few days later on his farm and before light I was on hands and knees in mud and sheepswallop digging a trench.

After day one he informed me that he could do with a hand around the place as he "had a couple of mobs to drench" I nodded acquiescence and snuck off to my well read and doggy eared dictionary to try and ascertain what the hell he was talking about.

I could figure out the mobs part as I was familiar with the lyrics of Black Sabbath and to my mind to drench would be ...to wash the bulls?? Who knew. I kept shtum and waited to see how things would go if I simply played it by ear.

Turned out that it means to either give an oral or poured on dose of whatever marvelously deadly chemical was on the menu for a number of differing ailments that bulls or sheep would suffer from and which would significantly alter the price they would be able to fetch when their lifespan had come to its abrupt and inglorious end.

It seemed simple enough. Problem was that the bulls had to be mustered from the paddocks and it was something quite new and a little strange for a person with such limited experience as myself.

Step one..mount motorcycle. Step two ride like hell through knee deep mud and do whatever it takes to get all of the cattle out in one group and heading in the right direction.

Simple!

Riiiight!..

First of all there was the problem of communication between the farmer and myself. He, taking for granted that , well..everyone grows up on a farm and knows instinctively what to do when it comes to such a simple task, completely and utterly omitted to give me any instruction whatsoever in the subtle art of moving livestock around.

The first few days were less than easy but to be honest..a lot of fun.

I grew up on bikes and love them. Needless to say I had no qualms about taking routes that led vertically down sheer cliffs or bombing through mud to head off a stray at the slightest provocation.

The farmer, being a gentle and kindly understanding soul, appreciated the fact that I was enthusiastic.......... although a little daft.

Probably due to my lack of meat.

This was a bone of contention between us as he would slide me a sidelong glance every now and again and inquire whether I was OK and didn't perhaps need some "real" food to keep me going. I think he was expecting me to collapse and wasn't sure what course of action to take if I did. CPR with a MAN!!! It would be bad form even if it was unobserved.

I of course managed to remain in a vertical position and at the end of the day when he was spent, I would have enough energy to cook, juggle and play my guitar before reading and bed. He would crash at about 7.30 and be roaring around on his quad before dawn.

Days turned to weeks and soon I had gained enough confidence to pretend I was a cowboy..or bullboy in this case and had honed my whooping skills to a fine luster and wasn't fazed in the slightest by the mud and mire that I found myself in for the entire duration of the day. It has been one of the wettest seasons in NZ and of course there was and still is mud up to your ankles on a dry day. A lot of work was done in the "yards" and this is a pool of pure mud, bullshit and urine that defies description. Not having wellington boots made the job even more fun and I would have crinkle cut toes before breakfast and they would stay that way all through the day.

Eventually..after about three days, my brand new waterproof leggings had completely worn through at the seat and so I would have a wet arse as well.

But it was great! I was running around on the bike and felt a bit like Steve McQueen in the Great Escape, riding around the hills.

There were times I was tempted to emulate him in that memorable scene where he jumps the fence. I restrained myself though as the little 100cc motor was way beyond sell by date and I would have ended up entangled half way up a deer fence that was electrified and didn't warm to the prospect. I doubt the farmer would have been impressed either.

The farm itself is situated in the Hawke's Bay region and quite close to the coast. It is a collection of paddocks that run along a river and not much more than a series of hills. It is a very, very pretty place when the sun shines and quiet and peaceful when the dogs aren't barking or the bulls bellowing up a storm. I have watched the full moon rising and saw orion for the first time this season in the middle of the night through the toilet window whilst taking a pee.

Many birds, rabbits, hawks and the odd possum that, if it evades the poison traps, simply gets blasted by the farmers trusty and well utilized shotgun. Much like Elmer Fudd...

There are Hereford Bulls for the most part. Black Angus and Hybrids as well as a number of sheep and goats. There used to be a few chooks too and a bloody noisy Cockerel but their numbers have dwindled due to the enthusiastic and successful pursuit of the dogs.

The dogs deserve a mention as they are simply..farm dogs. Meaning that they are here to work and nothing more. They spend their entire time locked up in their kennels and are let out only when needed.

Its quite an experience as an outsider to watch the farmer move a whole herd with his dogs just by whistling. It astounds me as he could be doing that but instead we tear around at breakneck speed and do most of it ourselves. But he is a solo operator and has run these 406 acres for 18 years on his own. It should be noted that he is in his 60's and limps due to two hip replacements. An amazing fellow to say the least and one of the most decent, down to earth and upright people I have ever had the privilege to meet.

I have observed him with a mix between outright curiosity and complete frustration. He is so old school it hurts. He has the whole farm in his head and although he may make a plan for the following day, it is forgotten at the moment he wakes up and then its a wild goose chase for the whole day while he mentally rearranges the "mobs" into suitable paddocks. He keeps all the numbers bouncing around up there and takes notes as to which have gotten what and when so he doesn't forget, and then loses the notes...Somehow he does an exemplary job and has the best looking bulls in the region by far.

How he does it is as much a mystery to me as my veggieness is to him.

Unfortunately he is a member of a dying breed.

New Zealand is famous for rugby and sheep for the most part and although there was at one stage around 75 million sheep, it is now an even split..more or less between livestock such as cows and bulls and said woolly ones. There is also a significant number of deer and a smattering of weird things such as Alpacas but they tend to be restricted to the more fringe members of the astronaut squad.

Wine is a huge industry as well and of course fruit that is mainly exported.

There just doesn't seem to be much interest in farming by the younger generation. I recently heard from an accountant that informed me that out of 240 odd farm sales he was directing, only 6 of the farms were being handed over to their sons. The average age of farmers right now is something like 60 or even 70 years old. The youngsters are not interested. I think its due to the fact that its really a lifestyle and hard work constantly. It takes an enormous amount of initial capital outlay to get into the game and the younger generation don't find it as appealing as being a gangster or some other type of occupation such as ...robber or..drug dealer and prefer for the most part to live on the dole, complain and basically create a nuisance of themselves. The smarter ones leave for Australia where there is work and ...Sun!

I don't blame them. Farming sux big time!

I don't have it in me to do this as a living. Although I have spent a considerable time on organic farms, it has been dealing mainly with plants of some sort. People who farm animals are a different breed entirely. They seem to be more extroverted than the plant guys.

I asked the farmer about that and he said that he had run an apple orchard once but found it sterile. He much preferred the interaction with "live" things. I could gather what he was getting at as I had noticed that animals have their own natures "sheeponality" so to speak and are not all the same. Initially I only saw the exterior but now as a seasoned pro I notice the lack of "condition" at a glance and can tell "good' ones from the rest.

What amazes me is although the farmer can spot a skinny lamb at 600 meters in fog, he wont notice the full and blazing moon at 4 pm or has any idea about the abundance of native plants on his property. Has little, if any knowledge about their uses and even less about what part they play or played in the lives of the Maori.

The farm is conveniently situated just 12 minutes from the closest town and although the farmer has lived in the country all his life he is as much a part of the current consumer society as anyone else. Its all too close to convention for me. But NZ is by and large a most old fashioned and conventional place.

Its not all a bad thing though, as these people, such as the farmer in question have still got a sense of honor that is wholly missing from the younger people and city dwellers in general.

They have a sense of decency instilled in them that is as admirable as it can be frustrating.

There are certain things about this way of life that I don't take to so easily. One is ..the killing. Call me a wuss but I don't like the idea of killing anything. I don't even step on ants, kill cockroaches or trap mice.

I have witnessed sheep having their throats cut and stood by whilst the farmer skinned and hung up the animals in the killing shed that were not salable and basically "dog tucker" What got my goat was the fact that there were two nearly born lambs within and I thought it a needless act due to the fact the it could have been solved by the simple operation of sewing up the extruded inside of the ewe, with no more than a few cm of wax thread that was not worth the effort to go to the nearby town to fetch.

Many small and may I say extremely cute lambs die off for a number of reasons and I find it hard to digest.

Its all part and parcel of life,. This I know, but I don't take to it. I don't judge it either.

Farming is a business like any other.

I, for my own part am glad to have had the experience of seeing these things up close and first hand. From the shearers who come in to "crutch" the ewes to the still moments when I would just stop my bike and sit and absorb the atmosphere.

I'm a richer person for it and am now quite certain..

A farmer I will never be!

Whatever floats your boat

One of the most ironic things about my experience with boats has been that it has all been on dry land.

Unless you count a couple of times across the English channel, I have not ever been to sea really. But...I've worked with boats. Boats are cool. I had a job once at the Tel Aviv marina and became aquainted with the nautical world of which I had often read but never really seen up close first hand. Well it was a baptism of fire in my case as I got to know those bloody Yaghts intimately. I started off by having to sand down the fiberglass with and angle grinder and spent my days sweating away in this stupid paper suit and being covered in millions of little fiberglass splinters which turned my life into a living hell. But I digress somewhat...

My most intimate and shall I say profound?..Yes, I shall. Profound encounter with a boat was also in Israel. On the very shores of the sea of Galilee in fact. The boat in question was over 2000 years old! Quite old for a relationship of any kind but most rewarding and fulfilling nevertheless.

It all started when I was homeless and wandering through the Basalt covered hills on the shores of the "Kinerret" as it is known and in search of a rather large and peculiarly shaped boulder. I made the aquaintance of a fellow rock hound and sometime sculptor such as myself who had a studio where I was to work for a few months whilst completing a commission for the city of Tiberias.

This particular fellow was not unbeknown to me and our first meeting a few months before was highly memorable as I distinctly remember telling him to "piss off!" Not an auspicious sign I have to agree but it served to embed the man into my brain as a total ninkumpoop and old fool who I did not neccesarily feel a strong inclination to meet again. As fate would have it though it was a few months later that I met him again and started a relationship that I can only describe as quite remarkable and one I was..should I say blessed? ...well Ok! Blessed to have had the privelage to experience.

The mans name is Yuval Lufan and what makes him extraordinary is not as you may have guessed, the fact that we both sculpt in Basalt and wander the hills in search of special looking rocks.(or as you may have secretly summised..I too am a ninkumpoop although not quite such an old fool but fool neverthless)

What makes "UV" special is the fact that he and his brother Moshe had discovered the only boat to ever be salvaged from the sea of Galilee that dated from the 2000 years ago.

It is a miraculous story and I am not going to go into it in detail here as it is far too long and can be read by Googling it so I will just give a basic overview of the whole thing.

Basically UV and his brother grew up on the shores of the lake at kibbutz Ginnosar and were sons from a long line of fisherman who had lived in this area for generations.

Both brothers are enthusiastic and active amateur archeologists and would spend their free time roaming the shoreline and surrounding hills in search of ancient artifacts. Both shared the dream of one day finding an ancient ship in the lake as no one had until this time managed to do so. The main reason is that wooden boats simply cannot survive in fresh water for any protracted length of time and so the only hope would be to find the metal bits from boats that were constructed much later on.

Now there is a legend of a "treasure ship" that has abounded in this area for yonks and is believed by every man and his dog in this region and beyond. There is some truth to the story as it was based on a real Turkish ship that sank with an army's pay on board or valuables, I'm not too sure. This was the ship that sparked the brothers interest and kept them looking over the years.

Now, one year the level of the lake had dropped to a record low due to the drought and so a substantially large area of lake bottom had been exposed providing the brothers with a veritable playground in which to hunt for coins and such, hoping for the big find.

And find they did! A boat dating from 2000 years ago was discovered completely preserved in a clay rich mud. The find was kept completely secret and experts were brought in to authenticate the date of the boat and then the excavation process was begun. It was spectuacular! Complete with a near war with the neighboring settlement who toted guns and tried to annex the find as their own to the intervention and assistance of the IDF to aid in the extraction of the boat.

The extraction of the boat took a few days and was executed by people from all walks of life. The kibbutz members worked in shifts round the clock to release the thing from the mud and to beat the rising waters of the lake. Press were there, visitors came from miles away and one enterprising man even set up his ice cream truck to supply the onlookers (who by now had to be policed) with refreshments.

The extraction itself was pretty miraculous. The wood was the consitency fo wet sponge and had no structural integrity whatsoever. To expose the timbers to the air was like pressing a destruct button and then the task of actually transporting the thing to a safe place was near to impossible. But it was accomplished!

The boat was encased in polyurethane foam and floated on the lake to the harbour where it spent the night and then moved to the specially built structure that contained a custom built tank and would house the boat in a special mix of molten wax for the next 14 years. This process was also quite a miracle as the technique was quite new and untested in the Israeli climate and monitored by people who had very little experience at most. But it was successfully accomplished and eventually found its way into the specially built exhibit in the Yigal Alon museum.

Now I come in ...stage left and dutifully following Uv to one of his countless meetings with visitors, VIP's, pilgrims and common folk who have come to the area and are not going to leave without an autograph from one or both of the discoverers. My job is to translate the questions from the film crew or Professor who is researching his book or whoever as UV's English is rudimentary and he struggles to understand the gist of the interrogation.. My Hebrew..well..sucks! but I have used English once or twice and so have been given the task of interpreting and learn more in one sitting than I would have with a paid guide. I learn that UV is the most generous and kind hearted of souls on the planet and also one of the most exploited. Being a member of the Kibbutz he has the responsibility of maintaining the many and varied gardens and toils away in the searing heat for most of his days. When a group or specialist or whatever comes along, he drops everything and heads off to tell his account of the discovery, answer questions, sign autographs and pose for a constant stream of photographs. This he does with great aplomb and as if it is the first time anyone has ever asked. It is rare that the visitor doesnt leave without a sense of wonder at the whole story and the man behind it. UV's brother has work elsewhere and so is less involved with the PR side and so it is UV who arrives back home to collapse in his chair and fall asleep completely spent.

Now as he is a Kibbutznik, he doesnt earn a cent for his activities and actually gets a lot of flak from some of the members due to his "celebrity" status. I was shocked to discover that only recently, due to the changes occurring in the Kibbutz system does UV get some kind of compensation for all his effort. Compared to what a standard guide earns it is pittance and the irony is that what the guides know they basically leart from UV himself or what was written up about the whole event.

Enter me again...this time from behind the keyboard as I discovered that although the brothers have a website..there is not really anything on it and the "main" site is actually controlled by the gift shop that is run by two rather astute businessmen. So I wrote up a couple of pages in English for them and in so doing once agian received a rather unusual inside look at the whole discovery story.

The boat itself has been dubbed "the Jesus Boat" and its the term it is most often used. To be more accurate as some more discerning people are, it is the "Ancient Boat" which really sucks as you cant sell curios using that name. The boat itself is one of a large number of boats used on the lake at the time and it has been calculated that there is a 0.06% chance that Jesus actually used the boat. Not a very high figure..much like finding a New York taxi and calling it the Robert De Niro taxi! Fact is that this boat is the ONLY artifact of its kind and as such it deserves every bit of credit that it recieves.

The boat is sometimes referred to as "the Miracle Boat" now this is in a strange way a term that has some credibitlity. Depending on who you speak to of course!

I have watched in horror as "pilgrims" have come on their Galilee experience trip and gone over to a piece of the boat that is encased in a glass cabinet and prostrated themselves or cross themselves a couple of times much to the derision of the onlooking staff who have seen far too much of this. Not so for the souvenir shop owners who it suits down to the ground. Many Asian tourists see it simply as another target that has to be digitally shot and filed away and an surprising amount of Korean Christians will show their devotion by making a small donation to the collection box. Others, such as the remarkable woman Professor who did the preservation will simply roll her eyes at the mention of a miracle, or the excavator who accepts that it was a remarkable find but considers the true miracle to be the self confessed athiest head of excavations going out on his own and offering a prayer to enable the boat to be succesfully "saved"

The boat is many things to many people and to me it was a catalyst that helped to form a strong bond with so many interesting individuals that I would never otherwise have been exposed to. The crazy and undeniable fact of the matter is that this damn boat has an uncanny effect on all those who cross its path. From its very first exposure to the present day it has acted as a "bridge" between people of all persuasions. The Yigal Allon center is dedicated to an amazing man who spent his life trying to forge connections with the local Arab population and the center was constructed to not only show the man as the top class General that he was, but also to highlight his work as a peacemaker. The boat in an ironic twist of fate has actually been extremely successful in the field of relationship forging.

UV summed it up so succinctly to me one evening when we had finished working on our respective sculptures..."to me this is the Peace Boat" he said..and turned to me with a smile in his eyes.

I thought back to our first encounter and had to agree.

9.1 km

Its exactly 9.1 km from the farm to the river where I park my car, not half a meter from the waters edge.

I take off my heavy steel capped work boots and peel off the filthy tracksuit pants I have been working in and change into shorts and sandals.

I have to walk across the submerged bridge to the other side about 30 meters away where I will hunt for rocks and then bring them back before taking them to the workshop and transforming them into the shapes I like.

I take a few steps into the ankle deep water and am struck by the shock of the cold water. A few steps on and I am aware of the swift current and slippery moss covered concrete that provides a makeshift road for the one or two farm vehicles that use this short cut to the local tavern.

Each step is absolute torture. I am not much one for the cold and this is way beyond my tough it out capability. Its like a kettle being brought to the boil. The intensity of the cold is almost too much to bare and escalates with each step. I stifle the urge to cry out at the top of my voice.

I make it to the other side and stand with hands on knees breathing through the cold and slowly making my way back through my un comfort zone to something reminiscent of normality. It takes a while. When I get to the point of simply burning I stand up straight and giggle to myself, realizing that I'm not really the rugged mountain man I would like to think I can be. That water was bloody FREEZING!

I am surprised as there is no snow covered mountain or icy feed to the stream that I know of.

I gather my wits and brace myself once more as I walk off in the rock blanket direction and step periodically into pools of water on my way there. It is no easier and so I try to keep to the tops of protruding rocks.

I am a rock hound today..my mornings work is complete and the afternoon is mine and I begin to lose myself in the sea of multifaceted rocks that are beneath my feet and surround me. Each one is unique. Each has its own spirit and character, just like a writer has paragraphs and words, the stone sculptor has rocks and writes upon them the letters as shapes and textures that tell their story in the universal tongue that converses with the soul. Sculpture.

I select two head sized stones and cradle them in each hand on my shoulder next to my cheek. I smell the mustiness and feel the cool wet against my skin as I walk like a double loaded shotputtist across the rocks towards the bridge and anticipate the journey through the icy liquid to the sanctuary of my car.

Its hard...... As hard as before and I shudder whilst resisting the urge to clench my teeth and purposefully breathe deeper and force myself to relax into the cold. It hurts. I manage to make my way across, preferring to distract myself by concentrating on each step as I take it. My Kung Fu training comes in handy as I slide my toes through the surface of the water to the slippery footing below so as not to make splashes and grip with my toes as I shift my center of gravity with each succeeding step. I get to the other side and drop the stones and without waiting return to the next crossing.

By concentrating on the steps I find I am less bothered by the cold. I begin to flow with each step and soon actually begin to enjoy the sensation. It is not comfortable but its no longer an agonizing exercise.

I find beautiful rocks. Some too big and heavy to take and I make a mental note of where they are for a possible future visit when the water level is lower and the weight can be transported more safely. Dark stones mainly, but with subtle variations. I don't know their scientific names and only know they are from inside the earth and volcanic. Two more and return to the car and dripping I make my way back home.

When I get to the farm I unload the stones and go down towards the new house just to hang out and sit on the deck in the silence looking at the tide come in to the river estuary. As I walk down the path I smell the fragrance of jasmine permeating the crisp rain cleansed air. Its an invasive pest but I don't care. I love the scent and it encourages me to breathe deeper. I sit on the deck and listen to the sound of birds and soon notice one or two rummaging through the leafy ground cover and others twittering and going from branch to branch in the trees close by. Some new visitors make themselves known too. Its spring and this area is on the migration trail and their bright plumage is a welcome sight.

For a short sharp moment I feel the stab of anxiety as my mind is crossed by a thought as icy as the river, 9.1km away. What if I am told to leave? What if I don't get a visa? How cool would it be to share this with my children so far way? When could that be? ....and then I relax again as a feeling of calm settles over me like a fine mist descending on my shoulders and penetrating my very bones. I become conscious of my being in the here and now and a smile creeps over my weary features. This is what matters.

Not tomorrow and all the plans, hopes, dreams and speculation, but herenow!

Fart gallery

Farts!

Don't you just love em?

They are unique, audible and feel good when you execute them with attitude!

Farts are one of the few bodily functions that have a built in olfactory bonus designed to benefit those with hearing impairment.

In short. Farts have power! Just think of the stink you can create when dropping one at the supper table or in court or the boardroom when an important decision is being decided upon. Timing is of the essence!

Society has developed a dis stinct bias against said activity. It is definitely not PC to do it in public and this has resulted in generations upon generations holding tight to the opinion that they should be stifled or suppressed in some way. What a load of..hot air..I would say. It's a medical fact that it's really unhealthy to hold onto one ..so to speak.

Hippies don't seem to care though. I recently had the dubious privilege of holding a slide show for a group of them and whilst expounding on the many and varied positive attributes to the art of building with mud, two members of the audience who may I say were very way past their prime hippie chicks simply let fly at will. It was most disheartening. Me being one to pretend that I am cool pretended to pay no attention to the staccato "pwaaaarps" and somewhat more basso notes emanating from what I could only imagine was a vuvuzela and a tuba engaged in animated conversation whilst being trapped deep in the recesses of the couch they were both sitting on.

Somehow the fact that it was two women gave me the creeps.

Now I'm sure you're wondering what got me onto this gaseous train of thought.

Well it all started when I was at the local city art gallery and looking at the "instillations" I immediately thought..."Ptah! All farts and no shit!" This is an expression I inherited from a Punk band called Omsepis from back in the day. They wrote a song about governmental promises that never ever came to fruition. It was based I would Imagine on the old joke/rhyme about going to the public toilet and paying your penny and only parting with wind. Feeling cheated if you like.

Well that's how I feel usually when I go to galleries and see the absolute ..poop.. that is being presented.

A bunch of coat hangers wrapped in toilet paper accompanied by a whole wall of theoretical nonsense. "Ooohh! Wow!" ....I HATE IT!!

Being a Sculptor doesn't help. I am always lumped in with these nondescript fools and I take umbrage. If that's the right word? I always thought umbrage was some kind of drink...who knows? Anyway...it's enough to drive me to drink as I am appalled by the state of the arts at present. There seems to be no skill involved and although I am not disputing the validity of the works, I do have my subjective albeit jaded view.

I do enjoy some instillations though. It is usually when the person is less than serious and the whole "persona" and "contrived eccentricity " of the artist is absent.

It's just a whole big ego trip for the most part and I am left thinking that there isn't much substance to fill the void...hence...all farts no shit.

Farts are more interesting and since I don't have the energy or desire to go out and actually DO an instillation such as this I have decided to create a literary piece of fiction. Every bit, if not more valid as a work of art than the non existent instillation that would have gone down in the anals of history were I to have done it.

So...

What I propose to do is to collect a series of farts. Literally.

Perhaps from celebrities and politicians, whatever. The idea is to "capture" their very essence in an appropriate container, seal it and put it on display in a gallery.

Now some people would have ornate glass jars and others, for example the head of the CIA may want to have it in a super secure, thermonuclear proof and unassuming container so as not to attract attention. Military types may want an empty shell casing or the queen would want pure crystal.

The single most important attribute would be the fact that ..well..farts are invisible!!! so only the container would give a hint as to what type of personality had deposited their well-earned gas into it. It's a paradoxical look at society and a melding between the macro and micro cosmos and all that twaddle...

People are like that though. Modern society feeds us the methane rich fodder that we should pay attention to our outer features and completely negate the fact that we are becoming creatures without substance.

Maybe it's what the powers that be want in the first place. Buy this and buy that and you will look good even if you aren't really good on the inside. Superficial and the way everybody seems to be able to want to relate to one another.

It all seems rather hal farted to me.

Anyway..the instillation idea is a sound one.....wait!

That's another dimension not yet fully explored. ...The sound!

It could be recorded at the time of deposit and could form an important side dish to the inert yet pressurized containers.

To take it a few steps further...there could be some musically talented audio whiz kid who could arrange an entire concerto using the material so liberally provided by the contributors. Imagine..Beethoven! Pwaarp Pwaarp Pwaarp Pwaaaaaaaaaaaaaaaarp! I'm sure you get the general idea.

Or even a live performance. The three tenors or whoever. Look!... watch my lips!!!...Nothing!

...And yet...!

Farts have yet another dimension to them that many a teenager has made full use of. They're flammable!

I once watched a guy at holiday camp who tried to show off and light one. He was wearing a speedo costume at the time and I must say he managed an extended and most impressive blue flame for quite a time before his swimming trunks caught fire, started to melt and the entire thing simply vanished into thin air. What didn't vanish were the seams and they melted straight into his skin! Boy did he scream! I loved it though, as he was a total bastard of a bully and I thought it was divine intervention to receive such a poetic form of retribution for his extensive list of crimes. It was a red speedo and I remember it clearly. All his fuzzy red pubes were singed too and I relish the memory of his pain and embarrassment.

But back to the point...imagine the fire show you could have! Total dark....Pwaaarp and Whooosh!

A sound and light show! I wonder who would have the bare faced cheek to choreograph it? I guess it goes without saying that the theater would have to have a fully operative air conditioning system as a prerequisite. You would also need performers who wouldn't simply run out of gas before the second scene.

I once read a story about a Tai Chi or Kung Fu teacher who used to follow a very strict diet to keep his "secret weapon" topped up at all times. I won't go any further into details except to say that the poor victims were, across the board immensely impressed if not a more than just a little nauseous at the mere thought of their unfortunate encounter. If he were a boxer I guess his ring name would have been Gaseous Clay! He certainly had a very different approach to Chi cultivation that's for sure.

But back to the artsy fartsy world of instillations and the like.

I think it's a great idea and wouldn't at all be surprised if it has already been done. C'mon..there was that guy who canned his own faeces and sold it!! Sold more than me anyhow and for a lot more moolah too!

At the end of the exhibition the works of fart could be auctioned off and the lucky and very rich person who purchases one will have the pleasure of either leaving the contents to mature or perhaps inviting friends around to savor the very manifest substance of the particular contributing donator.

Can you picture it..a bunch of oil sheiks around their gold table all waiting for their turn to sample the bouquet of perhaps the Queen or an African head of state. It would be a short lived experience too and perhaps a once in a lifetime opportunity. Possibly, with the intervention of some basic science, the effect could be sampled by more than one person by arranging the participants in a vertical fashion such as say standing on a ladder so the the rising hot air would not be dissipated so rapidly. That is of course whether the air would be hot in the first place.

Whichever the case, I think it would be a great theme and I would most happily welcome everyone to my "Fart Gallery."

Big Brother

Remember that Orwellian of all authors Orwellian, George Orwell? Well,.. or should I dislyxify that and say or well?...I always thought his first name should be Sick and somehow I also invented the fictitious name of Jawel Nofine that I would repeat to myself whenever I heard the name Orwell mentioned and I wonder now, as I did then what weird sense of association I have inherited from my gracious gene donators who have caused me to so grossly digress before I have even begun...

So.

The wonderful world that our Orwellian friend so Orwellianly and vividly described to us in the book 1984 was peppered with comments about one "Big Brother" who was the main baddie and had nothing to do for most of his time than to sit around drinking bad Gin and watching the citizens of his cleverly controlled world go about their day to day, humdrum lives.

This caught on quite enthusiastically in the 60's with t shirts and posters proclaiming "Big Brother is watching you" and in the blissful ignorance of my youth I had absolutely no idea of what it meant but thought it was cool anyway. Later of course I read the book for the first time and thought that the world being described was not that far from Apartheid really and so wasn't all that impressed to be honest. My second reading quite ironically I now realize in hindsight, was whilst I was in London in the very year 1984 and then went on to read Down and out in Paris and London whilst I was exactly that. Down and almost out in both of the cities only weeks after reading the 1984 book.

Well whats my point you may be asking at this point? Well, to put it pointedly I have to admit that I'm not quite sure just yet but as I continue writing, something should point the way and I am bound to make one or two along the way so be patient.

My point is actually connected to the use of cameras in our modern society if that helps you to bring the picture into focus. Now back in 84 in London there were already a huge number of cameras in operation in public places. They were eerie and mysterious things and provided great targets for empty lager cans and bottles of cider would make stress relieving sounds when striking the unit in its seemingly unassailable position way up on high.

Close circuit cameras were a common sight by then though and every good shoplifter knew how to evade detection and the more criminally adept would know that they were merely props designed for deterring crime than actually in operation. There wasn't someone at the monitor 24/7 and no one would be going over the tapes to check on shoplifters long gone anyhow and so were for all intents and purposes useless.

The cameras in operation at more official type places such as Buckingham palace were a slightly different story though and of course so were the ones at main stations such as Victoria for example. It wasn't wise to go around doing something dodgy in those kinds of places anyway and whoever was disruptive would soon be accosted by the plain clothes officers of the CID or their buddies at Scotland Yard who would smartly bundle them off to a more private location for a quiet little chat. Even back then the UK was already one of the most comprehensively covered countries on the planet and today is the worlds leader.

Its not only the "official" cameras that keep the population in Big Brothers watchful eye but the digital explosion has ushered in a new age of cameras that can fry eggs and have an indoor heated swimming pool and take better pictures than professional camera equipment could only a few short years ago. The most amazing thing about modern phones is that on top of all the other peripheral features you can actually use the device to phone someone and so when a crime is witnessed and recorded it can then be reported and the evidence sent in what is very close to real time to the authorities via e mail. This nifty little palm size wonder has put more people behind bars in a few years than the Pinkertons managed to do in 10.

It is a reliable witness and has perfect recall and whats even scarier, ..everybody has one. In some cases two or even three.

Its ironic to think that now that we have the most awesome tool in our hands in all of history, in the form of the personal computer and that we actually use these technological marvels that in theory set us free, to actually control ourselves as well. Its no secret that Television is addictive and that using the Internet is just as much or even more so. Our need to communicate from a safe place seems to be a lot more appealing than face to face conversations and already we see the trend taken to its extreme when people talk to each other on their cell phones whilst sitting in the same bus or restaurant or whatever. Just yesterday a friend sent me a message on his chat thingey while we were sitting only a few seats from each other. Admittedly he did it as a bit of a joke but in a way it served to illustrate the crazy situation we were in as we sat in a room full of people at the library all of us engaged silently in our various tasks and not as much as taking the slightest notice of the person sitting next to or opposite them. Myself included.

Those two little gadgets put together are as powerful as any kind of Big Brother that our Mr Orwell could have imagined. Possibly even more so.

Your laptop can be as good as a portable criminal record that has dates, times and details all neatly sewn up in gobbledeegook that is only understood by specialists and young people and whats really handy is that you carry it around with you and it can be accessed from anywhere by anyone who has the knowhow to do so.

The advent of all things digital is much like it has always been. A tool that can be used or abused. It is said that cigarettes don't have any harmful effects whatsoever. No coughs, no cancer, no emphysema, no bad breath even! Unless of course you smoke them. Like the gun, it is not the implement of death itself but the hand it is in that is at fault. Same goes for the propensity of cameras that abound and keep increasing wherever you go. They can be used to free lives or to control them and it remains to be seen which will be the dominant effect through the passing of time.

One thing you can be damn sure of though is that......Big Brother is watching you!

Punketory Lane

It all started on midnight, New Year's Eve 1976. I was stuck at home and was riding my skateboard on the concrete patch outside our house in Kensington, Jo'Burg.

I had my transistor radio tuned to Capitol radio and was having a good skate session in the warm summer evening with my shirt off and not a beer in sight. The music as usual was not what you would call mainstream and it was my station of choice since LM Radio had some time earlier bitten the dust. Everything was going fine with the occasional flying kick at the punch bag hanging from the Jacaranda tree and then my attention was grabbed by a song from the little transistor. I was mesmerized! WOW! This was some cool shit and I had not heard much like it before. Most people who think they know me would bet that it was the Sex Pistols but they'd be dead wrong as it was the band that that had made their own little splash in the European pond and were now swimming decisively towards the Ocean. The band of course was the Police. The song-—Message in a Bottle. I still love that track and feel like getting straight up from where I sit to play and record my own version on my palmtop studio!

The rest was all downhill (to understate things quite dramatically!)

I began my love affair with musik at a fairly young age and had been exposed to a pretty unusual variety of musical styles from an early age. My folks had a record player that I was of course not allowed to touch because I would "Scratch the records!" I was reduced to listening to whatever they decided to play and later what my older sister would decide to put on the turntable. Springbok Hits became the rage and my folks were not to be outdone by their friends and so began collecting the risky covered vinyl with a passion. Dan Hill also seems to be stuck in my memory, possibly because of the way his name was written with lightning bolts. All this was supplemented of course by a huge classical collection and the standard issue 7 singles like "Ag Pleez Deddy" and so forth. I used to explore through the hip high collection in the afternoons when homework should have been done and slowly but surely started sneaking tracks here and there while no one was home.

The change came when my sister hit her teens and started to bring back records she had borrowed from her friends and it was a wide collection of stuff. Hippy musik and Yeah Yeah Yeah musik as my Dad would call it. The Beatles were hot things to have with David Bowie bringing in the Weird and these records started to be "hidden" from the folks along with "Underground" musik. THAT was the total worst and one listen could turn you into a Heroin addict and Satan's slave with no redemption. So naturally these were the albums I gravitated towards.

I remember the first time I played Sabbath Bloody Sabbath alone at home. Awesome!! Even though I played it very softly in case the neighbours would hear and call the cops!

I mean ...you never know!!!

Jethro Tull and the banned Aqualung, Led Zep in all its unadulterated vinyl glory. T Rex, Cream, Deep Purple, the list goes on. A whole new world right there on my folks forbidden record player.

Eventually I hit 11 and for my birthday I ask for a guitar! All because I have listened to Frampton comes alive continually every afternoon for six months and can sing every riff. After much hassle my folks gave in and I get the little acoustic for 40 Rand! A fortune by anyone's standards. My Dad gets conned into buying the lesson book too and I go home and try to tune the damn thing up and TWANG!! There goes the first string and soon BETWAAANG!!! Two more. The guitar stays hanging around the house for the next 10 years or so and never gets fixed or tuned. It is years later that I figure out that I'm left handed and solve the mystery!! The trusty unplayed guitar gets its moment when I smash it over my head at one of our gigs many years later nearly concussing myself in the process!

For my twelfth birthday I get told I am old enough to get pocket money by the month and am allocated 12 rand for each calendar month. My first month and Saturday morning at Eastgate and I blow the lot on a cassette tape. Live and Dangerous-Thin Lizzy for 12.50. I have to fight for the 50cents advance on next month's salary and my Dad is totally disgusted at my irresponsibility!

Never mind the fact that I don't even own a tape recorder!!

Soon its time to go to High School and I meet up with someone who is into the Police and tapes me the first two albums. This is my musical staple diet for the next year or so while my musical knowledge grows towards more Hendrix, Ted Nugent, JJ Cale and Van Halen. The first two albums are amazing and I never go past a Greatermans or musik store where they let you listen without my usual dose of Jamies Crying and Talkin Bout Love.

While all this is happening it doesn't even occur to me that there may be a local musik scene.

One Sunday evening I return to the boarding School and realize that the next day there is a hair inspection and as I am not the most popular guy around, no one will cut my hair for me. Frustrated and shit scared of the caning I will receive the following day, I do the most logical thing under the circumstances and take a pair of scissors to my hair and create a most interesting imitation of a haircut. I'm instantly famous!! My hair stands up at odd angles and the headmaster is so amused/enraged that he orders me out of school to the barber to get it repaired and forgets the caning. Needless to say the hairdresser does his best but doesn't succeed in horizontilizing the airborne tufts of spikey matter.

I get the nickname spikey and all the shit that comes with it. Somehow it doesn't bug me since I am unaware of it unless I look in the mirror or see my reflection in a shop window.

The next step happens a few short weeks later when I am so pissed off by the situation at school that I take the phrase" We're treated like dogs!" to heart and attach one of our hounds choke chains to my neck by means of squashing the link in a vice and waiting to see the teachers reaction when I report to the swimming pool with a dog chain around my neck!! Permanently attached!!

The result was swift and painful and I was the laughing stock of the seniors when I had to saw it off in the Industrial Arts class. Unperturbed I then resorted to using a small Yale lock and removing the chain before PT class.

Soon enough some of the more radical senior boys started calling me "Punky" I didn't know shit about what they were talking about and the only thing I knew about Punk was a picture I had seen in the back of a Scope magazine of some guy with needles stuck through his cheek. I thought it was some kind of Indian cult! ....I swear.

Then one day someone called me "Hey Sid Vicious!!" and all his friends laughed. I went straight up to the skinny little shit and said "my name is not Sid Fucking Vicious!" I thought he would back down but the guy was ready to fight and we would have gone for it had a prefect not walked round the corner at the time.

To cut a long story short. This was my introduction to a small but tight group of friends who were into football and some pretty strange musik!!!

We inevitably became friends and I discovered that this Sid Vicious dude had a lock around his neck which was a well-established trademark in the circles that knew. I got my first taste of the Pistols and hated them! Except for the one line that blew me away..."Hiya boys I'm the chosen one. Can't ya fucking see!!" The most radical thing I had ever heard was the burp at the end of a Slade album and this pretty much kicked its butt.

I liked Ska, possibly a carry-over from the Police. Adam and the Ants was also a particular favourite. We weren't sure whether we were Mods or Rude boys or Punks or New wavers but we knew we were definitely NOT New Romantics!! They sucked!

At this point I had not yet been to any live performance of a band, much less a Punk band. The routine on Saturday mornings was to go to The Inner Sleeve and browse and listen to all the cool stuff they had. Sometimes during the week I would go to 55 Small Str. and do the same and enrich my encyclopaedia of bands that were largely unheard of and NEVER played on air. At this time I heard about a club called Bluebeat and used to steal my folks Volvo and spend all night at the club and get back just before dawn on a weekday. Needless to say I spent a lot of time bugging the DJ asking him/her to tell me what band was playing. Later the club became Metalbeat and I have a tear in my eye thinking about those amazing times all alone not knowing a soul, piss drunk and going nuts on the little dancefloor in my father's nightshirt that I had spray painted a few hours before in weird and wonderful shapes and designs. It was at about this time that "The boys" told me about a gig to take place at the Selbourne hall and a Punk band would be playing—-DOG!

I had heard about Dog and even seen them on Karl Kikilus's Pop Shop and played the tape over so many times that it eventually snapped. Antmusik was also on the program along with the Vapours turning Japanese so I got my money's worth.

Saturday rolled around and fortified with some Gin that I gleamed from my Dad's liquor cabinet and into town on an illegal motocross bike without a license. I made it in time to meet the boys and marvel at 'Chopheads" new tartan bondage pants. Finally got in and the hall was packed. All kinds of "alternative "people were there and I really don't remember the bands that played except for Dog. When they came on we had already fought our way to as near the front as we could and got to within "Gobbing" distance of the band. They came out and played and it was fucking brilliant. Everybody went nuts and it was unlike anything I had ever experienced. I left the gig with my shirt drenched in sweat and bumps on my eye brows from colliding with other people who no doubt had the same problems the next day along with strained neck muscles from totally losing it.

The most surprising thing for me was to see that there were other punks and were in some ways better informed than we were about punk music.

After that it was simply a must to see Dog whenever I could. The Asylum Kids were on the JHB scene too and had played at the Joubert park auditorium to a wild crowd and sadly I never got to see it. Apparently it was mind blowing and set the stage so to speak for bigger and better things to come. Unfortunately Punk was a byword for drunk wasted and vandalism so few if any venues were prepared to give what few bands there were or might have been the chance to play their brand of total noise. Punk in essence seemed to be more about the social chaos than the musik in any case and many would argue that it had no relevance in South Africa since it was a "British" thing and was for the "Pommies" Not everyone shared this view though and Durban seemed to have the best and most prolific scene. Could be since the then Natal was full of Pommies!!

Bands that topped the lists were Wild Youth with Johnny Teen and The Gay marines also making a fair bit of noise on their own. Ruben Rose, the drummer for Wild Youth eventually went on to form Powerage, arguably South African premier punk band in terms of commitment, attitude and the brutal raw power of their musik. The Durban scene in many ways was a lot more active than Jo Burg's and a few trips down to the coast were rewarded with a good night on the town and a decent enough gig to go to.

The Asylum Kids disbanded and Robbie Robb played in various different set ups looking for a niche and experimenting with various images and getting kicked out of pubs and so on until he got his act together and formed Tribe after Tribe with a Danish guy on the drums and although it wasn't Punk it was original and Robbie would always be relied upon to put on a damn good show and play some great guitar to boot.

This was just around the dawning of the 80's and the "first wave "of SA punk had been ridden and fizzled out on a pretty bare beach devoid of anything too interesting. E'Void and Via Afrika seemed to be the new trend and an "Ethnic" scene that was filled with upper middle class white students who were pretending to be black, dominated the pub/club circuit and bands like Jaluka with Sipho and Jonny Clegg were playing the stadiums to mixed audiences. They played in between making political speeches and the whole scene wasn't really conducive to spurning new talent from the streets.

1982 arrived and with it came the Exploited and the new wave of British and soon to be joined by US Punk rock. Gone was the creativity and experimental art school pop culture Punk Rock. The new musik was far more aggressive and simpler in many ways than the Punk of 77 England. Leather jackets and boots comprised the staples of the new uniform and no more were there tame little spiky tops. The Mohican firmly established itself as the standard cut and the whole original ideal of total personal freedom and individuality was lost as the musik became more acceptable as it became popular and the record companies started to take notice. For the most part though Punk was still the sound of the streets and independent labels sprang up like blackjacks on a highveld koppie.

In SA though, being a Punk simply meant that you were out of touch and out of date and a member of a minority within a minority within a minority within a minority. Not to mention that you were fair game on the street for any dickhead to come across with six of his buddies and kick your arse with relative impunity from the cops as those bastards would beat the crap out of you when you got to the cells anyhow. Many places wouldn't let you in if you were dressed Punk and the result was that the few people that there were around soon got to know each other and formed a relatively loose affiliation. The only place where Punks could go without too much of a problem was to clubs that would host Metal gigs and so the idea was drink up and make the best of it.

Occasionally a gig would happen and the one or two places would allow a Punk band to play would usually focus on a variety of bands. The Winton Joy Hotel in Hillbrow and the OX Box at the Oxford hotel in Rosebank were two such venues and they were primarily pubs. It was in Hillbrow where the so called second wave bands would play. I remember seeing Sulphate and Onslaught play at a Recreation centre run by the JHB City Council, as well as Dog Detachment who had ventured further musically and given vent to their fondness of Ian McCullough and Echo and the Bunnymen and were still playing various venues around the country. There were other bands not mentioned here that perhaps don't fit the Punk mold but were still "Punk friendly" to watch, such as No Exit who were a Mod influenced band and very close to the Jam in orientation. They played the coolest version of Booker T's Green Onions you ever heard. The king of clubs Pub in central JHB would also later host bands and notables were The Softies who were kind of Ska and The Dynamics with Steve Howells from the Asylum Kids on drums who played a mix of stuff somewhere between Ska and township jazz. Those gigs were cool as you could dance your arse off for two sets. No pub crawler worth his salt could finish this paragraph without mentioning Band of Gypsies. Hendrix clone guitarist and most of the rock classics and there you have a band that just were not aware that the 60's were over. They provided a great anchor when gigs were at an ebb in the flow and usually played loud and long!

But what about Punk!!!

Nada!

No gigs, no albums and no scene.

So I went to England!

I lived in a squat in London and ate from the soup kitchen with all the homeless in Thatcher's miner striked out UK. I went to all the clubs and pubs I could get to and stood around the backdoor offering to help carry equipment and so gain free entrance to the club. This was an old way of jumping the gate but after a few times that I honoured my agreement and pitched up to help after the gig I gained a reputation for being reliable and got to know some of the people I had been listening to for years. It got so that I actually roadied for Motorhead for two gigs but those guys were absolutely fucking crazy and with ice on the steps and no sleep weeks I thought it better to cut my career short before I dropped a amp stack and got my head kicked by the Hells Angels.

Back to SA, older, street wiser and 14 hole Doctor Martins with Belgian combat pants, a leather jacket and Mohawk and a new encyclopaedia of Punk in my slightly fried brain.....

Obviously the only thing to do was to start a band.

The first one was called Septic Lozenges. I was to join Ashley "Dorm" Braver on bass and Mark 'Pasta "on a kids drum kit. We practiced in a flat in Highpoint on the 25th floor and later they were to form a band called 1808 named after the flat number. We played some covers in our own way and the emphasis was on creating new material.

A few weeks later we managed to organize a gig with the original club owner of the premises where Metal beat used to be and played at the opening night of the club called Squatters. It was a chaotic first night. Our "Vocalist" was really nervous and had taken a handful of diet pills and was off his head and unable to play. I said Fuck It! and we got up on stage with our badly rehearsed and out of tune material and played to friends and curious that had come to watch the fun and games. I remember "The boys" all standing in the back who had come to watch what they always wanted to do but never did. I went berserk!!! Glam rock poses and jumps and eventually slid out on to the empty dancefloor on my knees to have my guitar cord pop out of the amp and I simply continued to play and pose unplugged!! It was great and the expressions on everyone's faces were priceless. Those that stayed anyway!!!

The club owner hit the roof and switched us off before the end of the set.

The Saturday night gig was totally out of the question and he kicked us out of the club.

Determined to play, we went to the club early in the afternoon and scaled a traffic light onto the balcony and passed our equipment up and waited with a few six-packs on the balcony until the cleaning staff arrived to prepare the club and let us in before the owner or management would arrive and throw us out.

Our amazement turned to shock and then horror as the club opened and started filling up with every kind of punk you could imagine. The place was totally packed and on an unavoidable trip to the boggs I was spotted by the manager and he came across and said "Hey! Get up there and play!" Needless to say we were up there as fast as we could manage it and played a totally blasting set to a full dance floor of pogoing spikey tops!!

I was in heaven...... I met so many new people that night and am still friends with some of them 20 years down the line.

After that there were one or two gigs at clubs where Punks would be hanging around outside and the management would let us do a set just before and sometimes while the other bands were packing their stuff. But on the whole we were in a pretty dead scene.

Soon, Ashley had to do his national service and as I suppose happens to many bands we simply faded away.

In the meanwhile I got together with the guys from Sulphate who had a new band called Midget Submarine and played guitar. We managed a few gigs and once played at the Dirtbox which was a so called Punk club that attracted all kinds of weird people who were ether fanatically Goth or something else and mostly young, ignorant and full of shit.

Drunk on the money that mom gave them.

More dry periods and then finally a gig at a new club that was prepared to have a punk night called Club Image.

Club Image was situated in the south side of JHB's central CBD district and was really a coloured club. Coloured people on one night and predominantly black on another and so it would rotate.

We got a gig for a Friday and if all went well we could play the next night as well.

Feverishly we set about making our own posters as usual and spreading the word and so played to a fair crowd on the Friday. Sat was less well supported and we left feeling relatively pleased that we had finally gotten round to playing.

It was on the Saturday night that I spoke with Martin, a drummer from my own area and told him that I wanted to make a separate project playing more hardcore musik. He was keen and although I took it with a pinch of salt, we organized to meet the following day and have a jam. I truly never expected him to come and it was with a sigh and a shrug that I went down to see if he was there as agreed upon. Much to my surprise he was and what's more he had transported his entire drum kit piece by piece on his 50cc motorbike!! I was most impressed. We jammed out some of the faster stuff that the guys in Midget Subs were less enthusiastic about and to my amazement he managed to nearly stay with me through the whole song. It was cool. We played some more and decided to meet again. The next time he arrived with my friend Simon who always said he wanted to start a band but had not had his own bass. He had borrowed this one from the bassist in Onslaught and was ready to give it stick. We jammed for a while until Simon's fingers were too sore and then planned a further practice later in the week. The next time we met was on our usual Midget Subs practice night and the deal was that we would play till the guys arrived and then it was Subs practice time. Well no one pitched up and an hour or so later , Joe the bassist for the Subs arrived with Pasta as backup and walked off with his amp in a huff!!

The next jam was with the addition of Simon's girlfriend's brother on guitar and he could actually play!! The jams were fun and we started sounding like something. My friend Jeremy Franklin took the vocal duties and sounded like Lemmy. Broken leg and crutches he would do the first gig reading the lyrics from a bundle of papers and shaking his fist in the air.

The following Friday I was standing outside the club waiting for the Midget Subs to arrive and it was getting later and later. Eventually the manager came out, recognized me and said" C'mon are your guys ready?' I looked at Simon and Simon looked at me and I said "Yeah sure were just waiting for the drummer!! Simon hopped into his car with Martin and raced off home to get all Martin's drum pedals and snare and stuff. We went on stage after exactly 7 hours of practice....TOTAL!!

The gig was good and we had more of a positive response with our original stuff than we had with the Subs playing covers.

Saturday night was fixed and we blew off the roof!!!

Toxik Sox was born!!!

Image was situated in a basement and with its garish black and day glow walls and smelly carpet it provided the perfect place for such a club. The club owner Roland Raker was a gemmologist by trade and ran the club side of things as a side-line to his "agency" which owned a few black and coloured acts and had a few notables like Brenda Fassie in his stable. With her it was more like a kennel as she was a poisonous bitch from the very first time I met her.

He ran things with "an Iron Fist" and it was on more than one occasion where I personally saw the results of such a fisty approach to owning a nightclub business in late 80's JHB.

He allowed us to play in his club though and got very enthusiastic about the punk scenes disregard for social convention and went as far as having one of his ex-cons paint a picture of Wattie from the Exploited on the side of his white Mercedes in enamel paint. Clearly the dude was hardcore.

Roland offered us a guest spot at the club but on Thursday evenings as it was possibly the quietest night of the week and the promise of the occasional Fri /Sat gig with other bands on the bill. It was winter and we were quickly sobered by playing out the entire month to the bar staff and captive audience of girlfriends and buddies. Frozen fingers and beer on the house and we slogged it out till a Sat gig with Carlos Dje Dje and his 20 odd band members known as the Prisoners. He of course was a Reggae act and there was a mixed group of races at the gigs. The band was getting better and soon attracting some attention due to the active graffiti campaign and very interesting walks down to the Star newspaper offices to personally do mail drops to the astonishment of all especially the security guards who would not let me past the door until I figured a way to give him the slip and deliver the goods to the pressroom before being manhandled and physically thrown out. It worked though, and soon interviews and snippets would appear here and there in the local press.

During this time we played and practiced at the club and basically didn't manage to venture out due to the tight hold that Roland exercised and the simple fact that what venues there were, basically were not interested in such a risky venture. Roland then offered us a "Contract" and in our enthusiastic naiveté we accepted as we thought that it would lead to recording the all elusive album that we all dreamed of making. All it meant in practical terms was that we were basically owned by Roland and whatever meagre and I do mean MEAGRE earnings there may have been was decimated to cover the list of expenses such as poster printing, equip. hire etc, etc, etc.

The band at that time was—ME! Looking cool, and playing the "V"

Jeremy on vox—Simon—bass Ricky—Guit and Martin on drums.

Everything was going pretty well and we had acquired a pretty solid crew of supporters that ranged from Punks. Skins, Head bangers, and assorted hangers on. We were far too rough for the Boutique type so called punks and appealed more to the gutter/ghetto types of which there were an alarming number.

We had created enough interest for some of the Durban bands to come up for a Punk gig and met some of the guys from VOD, Powerage, Screaming Foetus, as well as some JHB bands such as Omsepis and metal bands such as Ragnarock.. We were starting to sound really tight and definitely had our own sound and as I was continually writing new stuff our sets were becoming more varied and could handle two sets per night with not all the same material. Sadly the SADF stepped in and took Jeremy, leaving us without a vocalist and a precarious look into the future. We tried out a few hopefuls and it was useless. Eventually Martin succumbed to the same fate and we recruited Brendan from Omsepis as drummer as their band suffered the same kind of setbacks and were a few members short. I tried to do vocals in the interim and it was crazy since I couldn't sing and play at the same time and couldn't sing when I wasn't playing either. I went on a holiday with a new girlfriend and returned a few weeks later to discover that I had been "Fired "from the band by the newly recruited vocalist!!! I had never even heard the dude sing or been in a single jam with him but knew him from the scene. Antony or "Anti" as he liked to be known turned out to be a pretty good vocalist and front man and with him we went on to play other venues, record a song for the radio, win the battle of the bands, get beaten up in Vereeniging, play to a 7000 strong audience at Barney Simons alternative festival at the Portuguese hall (where Anti closed the gig and got the press by doing a stage dive at the end of the gig and concussing himself on the barrier in front of the stage!!) playing to a bunch of hippies at a club called Chango's and of course continuing our usual set at Club Image.

While all of this was happening the so called Alternative scene was starting to take off, albeit very slowly and gaining more attention and acceptance by the general public. No Friends of Harry along with The Psycho Reptiles were the main attractions and although not exactly mainstream, still managing to get gigs at the bigger venues such as the Thunderdome. It was obvious that if we were going to "Do" anything, we had to get on stage at the Thunderdome.

There was however a slight problem...Roland.... and the fact that his relations with the people from Thunderdome were very rocky due to obvious conflict of interest. This meant that we couldn't negotiate as we were contractually bound to Roland, and the Thunderdome people were less than anxious to talk to us anyway since I personally had a pretty rocky relationship with the management myself as I was known for "Bumming" the odd spare change from the people in the que's on Gig nights and had been thrown out for being too drunk or whatever a number of times by the meanest bouncers in town.

I don't know how it transpired eventually but I think that Simon, who usually handled the "business" side of things, was friendly with one of the Reptiles and in some weird way we secured a gig. I really don't know how it happened and wasn't interested. We were going to play THUNDERDOME!!! As a support act.

Many posters were made and distributed in the usual fashion (legwork and beer!) and the night arrived.

We were pretty ready and everyone was nervous as hell. My opening highlight of the evening was strutting straight up to the head bouncer standing at the VIP entrance and answering his" What can I do for you, Handsome?!!" with "You can tick of my name on the VIP list is what you can do, my good man!" and waltzed past feeling like a KING!

He would have killed me there and then if he could have. The expression on his face was priceless and now, writing this 20 odd years later, I feel a welling up of nervous emotion just recounting the incident.

Gotcha! Motherfucker!! Hahahahahaaaaa!

We didn't know what to expect. I personally never thought we would ever play the place to start with and to me it was like the culmination of all the honest to God hard work that I had put into this band and I was going to enjoy myself no matter what.

The atmosphere backstage was tense with all the others letting us know that we were a circus act and not to be taken seriously. I tuned my guitar twice and Brendan started lighting everyone's smokes to calm down (which was funny since he was a non-smoker) and a few minutes before gig time we just sat silently shitting ourselves.

We could hear the Crowd chanting..."Toxik Sox!..Toxik Sox!" and this over the attempted performance of the Psycho Reptiles. The Reptiles came back from the stage and Mike Searle was furious as someone had thrown a beer bottle at him and told him to 'Fuck Off!" they wanted Toxik Sox! I thought this was hilarious and pissed myself laughing as we walked up the stairs to the stage. Our act was started in unusual fashion by two really good friends Max and Cliff who were basically Metal fans and to my knowledge performed the very first live RAP on a SA stage. 'Were max and Cliff and we take no shit!' The opening lines I will never forget!!

Max finished the Rap and turned his baseball cap backwards, took a look over his shoulder at me, winked and dived right off the stage into a by now feverish crowd. He was followed by Cliffy and I took the que, looked at Brendan and we blasted straight into our set. I remember very little except that at some stage the smoke machine started blasting smoke at me and to escape being engulfed I moved forward looking over at Simon who was shaking his head and gesturing for me to look down which I did to realize that one more step and I would have plummeted down into the photographers pit a couple of meters down. The sound as usual was pathetic on stage and basically you just played with the drummer. It is what saved the night since I constantly would steal a glance across stage to Simon to see if we were playing the same song! Thankfully my Axe stayed more or less in tune and with the set over we left the stage and were mobbed by the people backstage. Roland was the first to grab me and was over the moon. Apparently we had played the best ever all though from our point of view it was more or less guesswork. One never knows! Gigs that I thought were great were received as mediocre and the ones where I couldn't hear a thing were dubbed as brilliant.

The good thing was that upon our return backstage quite a few of the previously reticent band members came up and congratulated us which was well cool.

The bad thing was that the video that I had left with the sound engineer to tape the gig was taped over and so the gig was lost forever. Stupid stoned Hippie! I did on one occasion listen to some tape that someone had recorded at the gig and at first I didn't even recognize that it was us. It was fucking AWESOME! And I'm truly sad that I don't have a copy to show my grandchildren.

We went back a second time to the Thunderdome and It was also a good gig.

At this time as mentioned before there still wasn't a 'Scene" as such. Making an album was pretty much out of the question due to the expense and minimal numbers of projected sales so in effect there seemed not very much more we could do.

The crunch came when Antony decided to leave SA for the UK and with him gone there want really anyone to fill his boots. I was having horrendous problems with family and pressure to work as well as drug use and abuse which finally culminated in me being sent through the courts at my parents request to a rehabilitation centre for six months. The irony of it all is that I saw it coming and had abstained from usage for the preceding weeks and if tested for drugs which I later was the results were all negative. Fact is that I was a disruptive element in society and vocal about my viewpoint in public as well as having folks that wanted to see their son with a suit and tie and respectable job with a future. All of the factors combined left me with little defence and so it was off for a holiday at the funny farm.

During this period I heard not a word from Roland or even a single call from the guys in the band although I got visits from people who would hitch hike from JHB to Cullinan after a Sat night out and come to visit me for Sunday visiting time.

After the period was done I returned to find that Simon had decided on a new project and the band was called Agent Orange. It was very much his brain child as ToxikSox was mine and I decided that it was a good idea to try to learn to play the guitar properly and focus on just being the Guitarist. Problem was that in my six month absence they had only come up with about three original songs and one of them was a direct rip off of one of my riffs. Nevermind I thought since my major intention with ToxikSox was to create a band without a leader or main man. My vision was that all forms of input would be accepted and everyone would be able to contribute. If it was going to happen with Agent Orange then it was OK by me. I was in fact pretty relieved that Simon had taken the creative initiative and included a Sax and Acoustic guitar into the line-up.

We did play again. Thunderdome, first gig, and at best it was pretty mediocre. I felt like I was back to square one and as I was skateboarding more I focused on that and eventually went to Cape Town.

It was finally over.

To conclude the saga......

This is my story as best I can remember it and the events and is to my knowledge as close to exactly what happened as I recall. The events didn't happen in precisely the order as the chronology of events is not 100% accurate. A lot more went down as you can imagine and it could fill a volume to recount all the anecdotes from that time. I have omitted many other players on the SA musical stage such as the Blast who we played with very frequently and other bands whose names I don't recall.

There is no particular reason for this. I am just telling the story off the bat as I do most things anyhow so no offence intended.

I'm now one of South Africa's few stone sculptors and I specialize in public works. I represent the country through my participation in sculpture symposia and travel all over the world and will do so as long as I am able.

I also still Freestyle and Slalom skateboard, competing in the Masters Division and make skate graphics for t shirts and decks. Whatever time is left is devoted to my Chinese martial art studies and of course last but not least ...family!!

I still play...Rhythm, Lead, Bass and now sing too. I write and record my own varied material on four track and have about 200 songs set to pre-defined drum patterns, all keeping my books happy on the shelf. God only knows what to do with them. My hobby is to invent new bands and then to post 4 songs on Myspace and I have 4 so far with more "ghost Bands" to follow. The musik ranges from Punk (there is a ToxikSox page with some of my remade stuff) Psychobilly, Ska, Blues .Stoner Metal, Power Pop, Acoustic stuff, and some of my own that I find difficult to classify. That goes under the band name—Brain Cell.

Will I ever do something more seriously in the musik dept.?

I truly don't know!

Capitalist punishment

I recently tried to access my emergency emergency funds that I purposely left stewing in my account in Israel with a dream like vision that if left untouched it would sit and accumulate interest and so when I needed it most I would have whatever extra on my 1000 NIS.

Ha Ha!! A dreamer I surely am.....

For starters I don't have Internet banking facilities or a credit card. My only means is to draw at an ATM or so I thought. I tried to e mail the "customer's service" number and sat for 20 mins whilst my so called options were relayed to me in Hebrew then Arabic and then Russian...NO English! I e-mailed again and was re referred to this number.

Eventually I got an Hebrew speaking person to phone up and try to figure out what to do to draw my much needed cash out of this convoluted institution. She phoned and we waited and eventually got to speak to whoever and then waited and then waited some more an eventually get to the point where they will ask me some "security" questions to ascertain that I really am who I am... After the mini interrogation I was finally transferred to some person at my branch that I supposedly would be assisted by.

Person in question does not speak a word of English and so the three way conversation ensues and it turns out that I am given a flat NO! When it comes to drawing my own hard earned cash!!! Why?? well someone gave me a huge pile of papers to sign (all in Hebrew) and of course I was assured that all was in order, but as is usual there was something that says I won't allow funds to be transferred to another account. A safeguard I remember being advised to take to prevent my account from being tampered with by the numerous institutions out there such as phone companies who have a habit of "mistakenly" charging you for services not rendered or requested. So....

I sit and wonder about the criminality of just one of an unending number of "official" capitalist institutions that day by day create situations that fleece you of whatever cash they can and usually by Non-Kosher means.

Let's simplify here for a second so my perspective can be clarified and my misconceptions and naiveté made plain for all to see.

I work for my money, I get paid, I go to a bank for "safe keeping" and as is the deal, they take some funds as after all it's their business too and usually the objective is to make money!

So I put my money in the bank to gain some interest only to discover that the bank is milking my account by charging me fees to have one. So in effect I'm renting my account and I can't get to use any of the simplest facilities promised..?????

MMMmmm...

The system is fraught with pitfalls for the person such as myself. I wondered about airport tax the other day. What is it for? How do I get an exemption? Hahaha!...When I asked I was met with the usual blank stare and a muttering along the lines of "That's the way it is!"

Who gets all that cash? It's a lot of cash too.

Prices steadily go up and salaries steadily lag behind. The list of questions is endless and as in all systems there are unending reasons to winge.

Where does it lead? What are the alternatives to existing in such a system?

Smash it down! I hear you say as I laugh in your face. That's ludicrous for too many reasons. Change it from within! Yeah riiiiight..

In my view its doomed from the start and failing as we speak so a viable alternative is more to the point .

What do we really need?

Besides the obvious such as food and water, shelter and so on, what do we really need as human beings to live a fruitful and fulfilling life?

Bucky Fuller once said something to the effect of.." A housewife needs to do no more than 20 mins of housework per day. Then she could spend more time doing something important like playing the violin!" I go with that sentiment. Fully.

With world population being what it is an growing as it does there should be no shortage of hands to do the menial stuff required to run buildings, cities, services and so on. Specialized work is of course not the issue here and I am not going to try and cover every aspect of a whole new outlook on life here so excuse me while I keep to an overview.

The basic point is hat we have the opportunity today to divide our time in such a way that we can draw a balance between "work" and "personal cultivation" as never before. Our technology allows us to accomplish things only dreamed of a few decades ago and we should be reaping the benefit of that but instead most of us are simply working away to achieve something that profits some other party and allows us to exist as nothing more than elevated slaves in a state of comfortable slavery. Too harsh you are saying.. Well think about it for a second. Or more if you like. Or don't you have the time?

Keeping a full time job, commuting , dealing with family issues, ablutions, meals and of course"relaxation" in the form of TV all take up your time and just to do this boring routine from day to day is a tall order in itself so where is the time and energy left for exploring a talent such as Photography, or improving your cooking...whatever. Things usually labeled as "leisure time" What the hell is leisure time? I have none. I doubt if you do.

Wealthier people in society are able to have more of this rare and elusive commodity and so the message is clear. More cash = more freedom. The catch is that to climb up the human pile you can not really do it through "hard work" which is the archetypal advice from all "honest hard working" folk who were nowhere near rich or in any hurry getting there..Most people today with piles of cash accumulated from scratch are exceedingly hardworking people, but perhaps with the exception that they chose fields of endeavor that were smart and lucrative. Smart in the sense that they found some sort of "job satisfaction" in the activity they chose. Most plod away as "the rent has to be paid y'know" and have their lives pretty much set in terms of vertical mobility.

You sleep one third of your day and you work for most of the rest. You save and go on "holiday" once, perhaps twice a year and for the most part its a simple necessity to recharge your batteries and get back to work. Round and round...some create a spiral and move either up or down but very few manage to bust out of their economic track.

Its all a bit dismal when seen from that perspective but not everything about capitalism sucks.

A Wall street banker once told me about his role as banker with people who wanted to "Invest Responsibly" It basically means that people who have made a lot of money, invest in some kind of socially beneficial venture. They not only pump their money into whatever, but do so with the intention of making a profit and then using that once again to finance their philanthropist projects. It is an example of how Capitalism can be used effectively as a tool to create additional wealth and distribute it into the community. The sad thing of course is that the mega buck fat cat daddy's aren't interested in that. They are out to feather their owns nests and gold plate the edges and damn the rest of you, and they tend to be the majority.

So back to the question of alternatives.

The question isn't new and since the 60's there have been numerous and varied attempts to create small scale societies based on wild and wondrous theories of how we can actually co exist in a society somehow.

Hippy communes and so on have projected an image of non descripts running naked around the desert and so on and we tend to have a uniformly jaded view on alternative communities of any kind.

Truth is though that there is a real surge of interest in alternative style lifestyles of late. Perhaps its a backlash against our current rate of technological change or overpopulation, but more and more people are seeking life outside of their urban roots and away from the current trends of our various societies .

Is technology outstripping human evolution? Who Knows?

One thing is clear to see though and that is that the people who try these lifestyles are always commenting on a kind of rediscovery, not only in terms of personal experience but particularly in the sphere of human interaction. Simply put. There is more. More focus is put on reconciling difficulties, decision making , etc. This is not only the result of communities to be small enough for you do do so but also due to the absence of Television which has all but killed the art of conversation and thus limited the potential for more meaningful interaction on a daily basis.

As a visitor and volunteer at Eco Villages in various lovely and not so lovely locations around the globe, I have had the opportunity to sample this kind of lifestyle first hand and my overriding impression is that these communities are more dissimilar than homogeneous. Human nature plays the most dominant role and initial idealistic zeal is soon lost/adjusted in the face of reality.

The places I have seen fall into reasonably distinct categories though. First type is the "Guru" place. One dominant individual shouts the odds or is at least more influential than the others and so things get done at the expense of possibly creating dissent in the group. Next is the "Social" place that has a core idea or doctrine that all adhere to and decisions are made by the appointed members of the group or the group as a whole based on majority vote. Once again there is the power play so typical of small communities and meetings take up more time than actual toil.Next would be the "Yuppie" place where the people can afford to develop and all is run rather loosely on a individualistic ownership based system. The list continues but thats enough to get the idea.

Question is? Which ones will survive?

Simple answer...I haven't a clue!

What I do know is that the Capitalist system takes us further from our humanity rather than bringing us closer. It tends to turn human beings into commodities and creates a judgment system based on only one aspect of the total person. It favors the minority and creates a situation in which strong can overcome the weak through ruthless exploitation such as we see in sweat shops and so on.

So I hear you all shouting.."So whats the bloody answer??!! . Do you want to see a whole world living "off the land" in little isolated farming based villages around the globe??"

Well. No! Not at all. I think there is no reason why the two cant go hand in hand. Hybridize! Discard what has been proven to be useless and nurture that which has. Take from anywhere, anything that would enable us as social beings to learn to actually live together! Because we haven't a clue how to do that as a species and a little practice is in order.

Set up "experimental communities" with funding and resources and lets see what it is that actually makes us tick and how we could tick in harmony, side by side without going BOOM!

Put education further up our list of national priorities and perhaps re evaluate what and how we learn stuff.

Its not a Utopian view at all.

Its not Utopian pie in the sky to want to have a life in which you are able to work and contribute to society and have time to play, in which you are able to develop, and I am not talking about 30 mins of squash twice a week! Where you are able to "learn" is what I mean. Be it perfecting a skill, reading or whatever, the idea is that it is still"work" but not as in..production, deadlines and so forth. Its not entertainment either. Thats a different kind of activity/inactivity.

We have had the concept of personal cultivation so badly relegated down our list of "to do" things that it is seen as pure luxury when it is a more like a birthright! "theres no time for that!" You say..Well...no there isn't!! Go figure? Why don't you have the time?

Isn't it *your* time after all?

100% proof

Although I am basically an unemployed, homeless and poor, I lead a rather rich and eventful life. I tend to prefer things of the spirit although have no aversion for dollars whatsoever and none of the clothing in my backpack clashes with that particular shade of green.

Spiritual things fascinate me and I am an avid watcher of all things spiritual such as Nuns, Priests, Monks, Volkswagens and the occasional Guru. I love visiting Old Churches and am in awe of the old Gothic cathedrals with their buttressed up buttresses and overly ornate stone work and decorations. The internal spaces in particular are a definite spiritual place for me and it's my favourite venue for my activities as a spiritual watcher. It's a kind of arena and I marvel at the pious expressions on the faces of the devoted and the quizzical ones on those of the camera clicking tourists. Churches are a really special place for me and I always get a weird feeling in the older ones. I asked my Monk friend about this once and he explained it very clearly to me. "The reason for that feeling of power is due to all the prayers that have over hundreds of years become embedded in the actual stone of the building" Well who can argue? It's obvious when you think of it. I have also had the distinct privilege of being able to watch the ultra-orthodox Jews in Old Jerusalem praying at the famous "wailing wall" That's a place to be awed for sure. There are these guys wearing furry cake tins on their heads with pants tucked into sox and heavy jackets in the 35 degree heat. Happily sweating away like any other animal besides the pig as they aren't Kosher and stinking to high heaven as they don't wear deodorant of any kind. Straight out of the 14th century and talking to one another on their cell phones at the top of their voices as if no one else exists. To them, I wonder if they actually can see members of the rest of the human race or whether it has been evolutionarily removed through years of not paying attention and sharing the ever decreasing gene pool. The separation between males and females was something that I found hard to deal with at first but it was the separation between the various Christian factions at the Holiest of Holies, the Church of the Holy Sepulchre that I found hardest to deal with. I noticed that the choirs would be singing and have shifts to do so. What I found out from one of the guides and then verified later through other sources (you have to take a guide who tells you dead pan, that the falafel stall you're standing at was where Jesus ate his last falafel before making his way grimly to the spot marked with a cross, with a liberal sprinkling of salt!) ..Anyway...it turns out that the priests have been fighting with each other for years as to whose duty it is to polish the small 18 x 10 inch step leading into the church. So much so that people have actually been killed in the struggles!! Now they have agreed that they will enter the doorway from one end and then leave in an agreed upon direction so that the next shift will not have to contact the previous one. This seems to be the best situation as they dont have the chance to bust out into fully fledged battle as they pass one another.

I haven't been to India yet and I believe that's a pretty cool place to check out the spiritual ones. A bit like the Olympics in terms of spiritual watching. From what I have heard it seems to be a little similar there too. I have to admit though that there are too many different factions for me to even pretend that I know the difference so I won't go there except to say that it seems that one common demon-inator with the spiritual ones is that they can't stand each other. The Shiites like their eggs Sunny side up and the Hindus feed the cows before their kids and the Jianas have a cool name and the Brahmans and Sheiks and the list goes on and on. It's all too confusing for me.

What happened to God? Well that's a good question. Originally the whole idea was to worship the Almighty and none other before Him, except of course if He came down to Earth in the guise of a human bean. That's where things go awry and the beans start jumping and jiving as to whose interpretation is correct and was it Avira or Jesus or Mazda or Mithras or Buddha or all of them?? I have to ask why God would want to come down here at all in the first place even less as to what he would want. Now when I mention God here I dont mean the dude with the long white beard sitting on a cloud cos that's Moses from what I'm told.

God is such an ill-defined entity in the first place. I speak to Christians and Jews about this quite a lot and common consensus is that there is none. Some have a world view which holds that God made the Earth and everything in it in 6 days and rested on the 7th. Others say that He is concerned only with this planet and that there is no life elsewhere whatsoever. Others seem to think that God is pure energy and permeates everything in the entire universe. Many things have been put forward, pure light, divine energy in the form of Man, etc, etc.

The Buddhists dont even mention a God at all.

Satan is of course the seriously baddest dude of all dudes and dudesses. He likes it HOT and if you dont play the game you're toast. There is a lot of dissent in the ranks as to what the Devil is as well. I'm not going to go into detail but it is all BAD and even my more fringe oriented contributors to the various discussions tend to agree, except that to them Bad is Good! ...Go figure.

The only seemingly common ground is that the human race tends to have had and probably will continue to have a concept tucked away in its murky recesses, a concept of some "Higher' being and I'm not talking about the boss. All cultures besides the possible exception of the one I haven't yet heard of, has at some stage or another all had a concept of spiritual beings. The Chinese have done a great job, as have the Indians who besides having brought the divine gift of Curry to the world and of course the mathematical concept of Zero have a whole planet of Gods, Goddesses, minor Gods, Angels, Pure Evil Parking attendants who drag you off to a millennium of reverse parking and legions of other non-descript other worldly beings. Legions!! Now that's a lot!

So..Where does this leave us in our new digital, all seeing, all knowing world? Will God evolve to keep up with the changes? Will the Bible, Koran, Torah and Hitchhikers guide to the Galaxy all be updated to accommodate the new developments in the fields of Science, Technology, Warfare; Computer aided Design and Electronic music? Or perhaps the question should be plonked on its head. Will Man evolve to accommodate a fully up to date and super futuristic God? Will the planets population actually reach a spiritual common ground? I mean, let's face it. There has been no better time in the entire known history of our kind. Already that's an assumption..."our kind" I wonder what "our kind" actually is. Perhaps we are not all from one source? Maybe some were evolved from apes and dolphins and others due to interbreeding with aliens. Whatever the case may be we still haven't learnt to live with each other even if we profess to share the same core values, as our history has proven countless times over.

I have often thought about what it would be like to have some kind of compound that would cause instant amnesia. Just temporarily of course. That way all the ongoing conflicts like the Middle East for one, would be able to be overcome. Man would still have the inbred urge to worship something higher and Devine and so I would build a huge Temple in Jerusalem or even better in a brand new place where people could come and worship the one God. Without fear, prejudice or restraint.

A little Utopian you may argue and if I were to return to the solid ground of Earth I would have to agree, since it seems Man also has this inbred urge to control his environment and that means others that share his environment. The urge to dominate and exploit seems to be just as deeply rooted if not more so than the urge to transcend his animal nature.

A bit dismal if you think about it too much so I adopt my much used and abused Zen training and I "dop it".....uh..I mean "drop it" and watch while the miracle of life unfolds in front of my eyes and I marvel at the wonder of it all.

Fight war not wars

Sitting in the bombproof box. Listening or rather feeling the katyushiot rockets strike the earth. The sound is "Ka Rump!" and not "Boooom!" like I imagined at first. Its not dark. On the contrary. The room is lit jail cell style with stark white lights against the even starker clinically white, cheaply painted walls. I wonder what blood would look like splatterred up against them and then catch myself as I look at the children playing monopoly and the parents, mothers mainly, feighning unaffectadness by the world outside. Their over attentive participation gives their true anxiety away. But only if you look closely,...... and I am.

I am the only adult man. I regularly go up the stairs to fetch water and ventilation fans and pancakes and basically anything that I can to show that I am also unaffected by the world outside the solid steel door. The shelter is basically a concrete subterranian vault with a heavy, lockable and sealable, safe door. The air is stale and the atmosphere pregnant....8 months plus.

The siren sounds and the relief is palpable. Everyone makes their way outside to the steaming hot day to continue with their lives before the siren sounds again and there is the rush to beat the 45 second window between warning and impact.Everything is exactly as before and life continues....

On the other side of the fence, a short 30km or so away things are much the same except the danger far more extreme. The air strikes are targeting the guerrilla strongholds but they are nothing more than basements or first floor rooms in an urban block of flats. The deviding line between civilian and combattant is non existant to the untrained observer and the underground network of tunnels and bunkers that hold personell and weaponry invisible. One thing is identical between the mothers and children of both sides though and that is the inescapable fear that goes with holing up in the ground while under enemy fire.The airstrike is over and those that are able, make their way above ground to survey the remains and proceed to continue with life as usual....

I, for my part watch the news for the first time in my life. I bounce between Sky, CNN, BBC, Fox and progressively get more and more pissed off. Each highlights its own take and the closest to an objective view turnes out to be Fox News. It's an absolute circus. "Watch the war on TV at the following times...."I get more pissed off. Israelis are depicted as war hungry ,over enthusiastic, sadistic oppressors and the Lebonese as victims of a cruel and unjust campaign of destruction. It kind of gets to me since I share the shelter with Mums and kids who are constantly fearful for their husbands and fathers. People I know from walking to my studio and driving past the playground and picking up my kids from the kindergarten and one thing is sure....soldiers they are not. Military service is compulsory for all young people in Israel. Boys are expected to do 3 years and girls 2. It's not voluntary. The case across the border I can only guess at. The people who are launching rockets at civilians are the same that put bomb factories adjacent or more commonly directly above or below their childrens schools and hide amongst the general population. I am in no position to be a judge... Except that as a breathing human being I reserve the right to condemn both actions as absolutely disgracefull. Violence breeds violence. I dont take sides at all. I cannot. I am dumbfounded by the way that life still just goes on as... normal.....

Politicians all have their say. This side....that side all from moral high ground created out of their own personal pile of bones. I get more pissed off. About as annoyed as those that attend the various anti war protests across the globe in the democracies that tolerate such behaviour.The anti war protests in Israel are less well publicised in the press. The support for this war however is well across the board though. Even the notorious peace loving pacifists come out in favour of Israels decisive action. I am confused and angry. My children are now sharing the floor of my brother in law's floor with my wife, on an inflatible mattress while I get the whole couch to myself. I'm not complaining because by all accounts we are one of the more fortunate families as I am not obliged to do military service.

This whole event comes in the wake of the recent world cup football competition and it's a time that I set aside to spend with my young son , who like other 5 year olds are taken up by the fever surrounding the football frenzy. It's a little more difficult for me to explain to him that "the War" is not another competition. His religious friends have explained to him that Israel will easily win because God is allways on Israel's side. I get more and more pissed off. I wonder how parents on the other side of the border approach this subject. Needless to say I try to attempt to explain to him what I perceive is the truth and at the same time am painfully aware of how far off base I could be.

It perplexes me because I dont want to spawn a soldier. Not that kind anyhow, but that's another story.

.......Still life continues as normal.

The cool thing to come out of this is that I manage to get into the shelter which is usually out of bounds. It's a good place to play my guitar and practice new songs and the war provides me with a small body of songs on my acoustic guitar. I also manage to practice some stationary freestyle skateboarding tricks while most of the residents are away in the safety of the center of the country. It is not too long after though, that I have to go to Tel Aviv and join the million plus people that have fled the northern region of Israel for an undefined time. In Tel Aviv things are actually quite quiet and life continues as normal.....

The bonus of all this is that many things now become free for residents of the north. We go to movies and parks and there is no need to pay the usual fees. It's OK except that it continues for an indefinite time and soon the kids want to go home and so do we. Meanwhile the Lebonese are being pounded. Pounded and pounded. The daily count for rockets coming over the border into Israel averages out at about

100 a day at a rough estimate.The villages nearby are hit . ALL of them suffer some kind of damage. There are casualties and broken hearts but nothing out of the ordinary.I still continue to watch the news and am progressively becoming pissed off. A newsflash!! Airports are closed as a terrorist plot to blow up planes is foiled. I listen to the people complain about their discomfort and the new security measures at the airports. I laugh as this is what we in Israel are all used to in what is considered peacetime.

Life goes on as usual...

Finally it breaks.....Ceasefire! We can finally go home and wash the 30 day old dishes and reclaim our living space from the cocroaches that have taken advantage of our absence.We have to throw out overything and re-pack the house as it has become a haven for scorpions and centipedes.Goodbye to the garden that was unwatered for a month and hello to long lost neighbors and the community.Try to get back to normal....

Now should be the time for the much anticipated war stories , but strangely there are none. People want to move on. The swimming pool re-opens and families take advantage of the "quiet"....Too quiet for me though. I am now home and dont keep up with the news. Thing is that it is REALLY QUIET!! Usually our days are punctuated by the sounds of helicopters and the odd day or two per week when the jets practice and dog fight and chase eachother at low altitudes throught the Galilean hills that I currently call home.None of that. Just the birds on their bi annual migratory flights and the new vegetation announcing the close of summer and the rapidly approaching autumn. Life seems to be continuing as usual...

Until the next one

The three medium pigz

Once upon a time there were three medium pigs. They were rather well to do yuppies and consequently could be broadly described as being somewhat portly and well hoofed.

Being the good friends they were, they decided one day to take a well earned break from their day jobs at the bank and stock exchange and got together to spend a weekend out of town in a secluded forest not far away.

Well!...they had such a cool time that upon arriving back at work on Monday morning they each set about checking up on real estate prices in what was known as "Howling Wolf Forest"

It was amazing! The prices were soooo cheap! So each individually bought up as much land as they could for a snap and before the phone had managed to cool off, they quit, packed up the 4 x4 and headed off to start brand new lives on the other side where the grass was always greener.

Soon after arrival it became clear that shelter was the top priority and so they sat down to discuss the building methods to be employed. After much heated debate they succumbed to the common result when having a decision making pow wow..... Disagreement!

The result was that each, thinking that he had the best method, exercised his Democratic right to choose and so went their separate ways.

Pig #1 opted for minimal labor intensity and speed of construction and created a makeshift shelter out of straw. Soon, said pig was happily relaxing outside his completed dwelling in his deck chair when he heard the ominous sound of heavy,.... ooohh!.. VERY HEAVY footsteps approaching.

Being the cautious and cowardly type of pig that he was, he wasted no time whatsoever and ducked into his straw hut and reluctantly peeped through the generous gaps in the walls where he had so soon before cut building expenditure by skimping on straw.

When he saw the creature come into his sloppily cleared clearing he jumped with fright. Not very much of a jump you have to understand, as he was rather the portliest of the three and was well attached to Earth by gravitational force as first described by Sir Isaac Newton way back when.

It was a good jump nevertheless and no sooner had he landed on Terra Firma when the creature politely knocked on the rapidly disintegrating front door. "Uhhh, Hoo izzit?" squeaked the pig whereupon the response was swift, confident and rather suave...."It's me! Howlin Wolf of Howling Wolf Forest! Would you be so kind as to let me in?" "NO!....I'm afraid" said the pig in a pathetic little tremor. "Oh no!.... Here we go again" sighed the wolf with a visible trace of tedium which he immidiately snapped out of by by snapping "OK then! If you don't lemme in I will huff and puff and blow your little shack to hell and gone you silly little unKosher excuse for a mud wallowing mammal!!.... and by the way you don't need to be afraid" Well, the pig sucked in a deep breath, waited for the adrenaline spike to subside for just a second and then ran like a fat bat out of hades straight through the skimpy wall of his shack and was lost in a cloud of dust.

The wolf, too startled and amused at the sight to give chase, simply giggled and set off at a leisurely pace in the direction that the pig had taken off in.

Meanwhile, Pig #2 who had decided that sticks were a far more viable building material than straw had been toiling away all day and was just adding some finishing touches to his small yet aesthetically pleasing and rather rustic in style twig and stick Yurt, when a disheveled looking #1 Pig burst through the undergrowth and too out of breath to scream, flew right past him, straight into the Yurt and slammed the door so hard behind him that the whole structure shook and shuddered for a full 16 seconds. The #2 pig stood for a moment and then did the most logical thing and ....knocked on the door. An out of breath little peep came from inside the newly completed construction "hah..heh hah..heh hah..heh..uuhh...hoo izzit?" Its me! #2 Pig" said the pig with as much aplomb as he could muster. " Uuhh...What do you want?" Said Pig #1. "I would like to enter my new home if it isn't too much trouble" said Pig #2 "Uhh....OK!" said Pig # 1 realising that he felt a little lonely in there all alone and could do with the company. So carefully unlocking the door and sneaking a quick peek to check if it really was Pig #2, he let him in and once again locked the door behind him.

Now, Pig #2 was more than a little curious and was about to ask Pig #1 what was going on when he was beaten to the punch by the sound of....oooh!.... Heavy,...VERY HEAVY footsteps coming their way.

It wasn't long before a familiar scene started to play itself out.

A heavy knock on the door followed by a more assertive reply than before. "Who is It?" asked Pig #2 quite assertively. "It is I!" said the wolf " May I introduce myself? " I am.." "I KNOW WHO YOU ARE!!" bellowed Pig #1. Much to the surprise of the wolf and Pig #2 who had never ever even heard Pig#1 as much as raise his voice. "Now wait just a second!" Said the Wolf rather irritably. "You are not following the script my dear fellow! And I will not allow you to steal this scene so LET ME IN! OR...."

"Or what?" asked Pig #2. "Um...Oh! Or I'll huff and I'll puff and blow your house DOOOOOWN!" Growled the Wolf in the best rendition of a fierce wolf's grauwl he could muster. "Wow!" exclaimed both Pigs in unison " that was awesome! Well done!" The Wolf, quite flattered by the compliment and well chuffed with his growl beamed with the praise. "Aha!!" Said Pig #2, (and I quote..) "Not by the hair on my chinny chin chin!....so there!" The Wolf took a HUGE breath and I kid you not, he blew that twig shack to smithereens in one breath! WHOOOOOOSH!

The two Pigs stood dumbfounded for only a moment before running like two fat bats out of hades into the forest, leaving only the distinctive scent of smoked ham in their combined wake.

Now, let us pause for a few moments and investigate what it was that Pig#3 had been up to.

Pig #3 was a remarkable porker and had decided that a conventionally built house was out of the question. He was of the opinion that some form of alternative building method should be employed to minimize his carbon footprint and thus minimize his impact on his local biosphere and thus minimize his detrimental impact on the planet as a whole.

To achieve this he had gone to great lengths to construct an ecologically responsible dwelling that used a geodesic dome skeleton covered with straw bales and finally plastered over with mud from the region and a special mix of lime based plaster as the final coat. He was just administering this coat and about to stand back and inspect his work when he heard the approaching commotion and noticed the cloud of dust that spewed forth behind his two comrades as they hightailed it out of the forest towards him.

They came to a screeching halt in front of him and simultaneously started to jabber incoherently in between gasping for breath. The Pig was a poor sufferer of fools and duly screamed at the top of his lungs at the blabbering twosome "SHUT AAAAAP!" The both of them were startled into silence and stood staring as the sudden silence served to amplify the underlying the background grumble which soon became more prominent and it wasn't long before it was well into the foreground and playing a protagonistic role.

Now Pig#3 had read the script beforehand and so knew exactly what the source of the ominous footsteps was. "OK you two. We'll sort this out later but meanwhile lets all get inside and lock the front door" Like a flash they were within the safety of the mud and straw bale walls that were reinforced with the underlying geodesic structure and waited for the Wolf to take his que.

The Wolf duly arrived and proceeded to knock on the door whereupon he was interrupted by Pig#3 who informed him that the story was limited to 3000 words maximum and so lets skip the preliminaries and go straight to the HUFFING and PUFFING part.

The Wolf, being lazy and quite tired after his stroll agreed without complaint and so skipped to the correct pick up point and without ceremony proceeded to blow his heart and his lungs out for as long as his breath lasted.

Of course it goes without saying that a structure such as this, being the safest way to build even in seismically active zones suffered not the slightest damage, but we will say so anyhow. In fact the high velocity hot air stream converted some of the imperfections in the plaster into a glassy smooth ceramic glaze like finish which Pig #3 immediately noticed and being an Autodidact duly recorded in his notebook as a new discovery and left it there for future reference.

Whilst the Wolf got his breath back the whole story moved straight out of the final scene in that act and directly to the first scene in the second last act.

So...here was the Wolf, having just regained his breath and being slightly hyper ventilated, wandered around the house looking for a different way to get in. It was clear even from a distance that the Wolf was very impressed with the workmanship and had to catch himself short when he was about to give the Pig a compliment as it would have compromised his macho image and besides it wasn't in the script. He thought of a wide array of adjectives to adequately describe the building in question and finally settled on the highest praise he could think of and although it was an idiomatic phrase rather than an word, he silently exclaimed to himself..."Sweet as Mate!!"

Finally, he eventually got tired and decided to take a nap as the Actors Union clearly stipulated that all registered members were to take regular breaks during performances and made himself comfortable nearby with a good view of the house in case an opportunity presented itself and he could act quickly to take advantage.

The three Pigs were now trapped in the house and had not yet stocked up with enough supplies to withstand a prolonged siege. It was clear that they would have to find some way to scare the Wolf off, even if it was temporarily.

Now #3Pig, being by far the brightest of the three, had as we have already mentioned, taken the liberty to read ahead and so got cracking with boiling the water he needed for the next scene in his solar kettle. It wasn't long before the water was boiling happily and the steam pouring skyward through the immaculately constructed chimney. The Wolf was fast asleep and about to miss his que so the three started banging pots and pans together in an attempt to create enough noise to wake the slumbering beast.

Upon awakening from a lovely dream of a bumper meal of pork chops and chips generously dressed in ketchup and served with fresh herbs and a glass of slightly fruity, yet full bodied but not overbearing Chianti, the Wolf immediately noticed the steam issuing forth from the immaculately constructed chimney and made the necessary calculations by means of traditional deductive reasoning to reach the conclusion that if the steam could come out he could go in.

He climber right up the newly set plaster and dove feet first down the chimney. He landed in the scalding water with a resounding splash and Loony Tunes like, shot straight back out of the chimney and scampered of yelping into the forest with a sizzling butt leaving a misty, ethereal trail along his chosen path.

The three Pigs rejoiced loudly and longly and then they took their nap due to the Unions regs, blah, blah, blah.

Much later they awoke and as it was with Pigs from all nations they were ravenously hungry and began preparing a healthy vegetarian meal. They ate, drank and were merry and went to sleep once more to be rested for the next morning when they would wake up and sit down and hammer out an agreement that was acceptable to all and would lead to the establishment of the first Ecologically oriented Democratically run, semi Capitalist, multi denominational Commune in that neck of the woods.

They had learnt a lot during their ordeal and besides saving their own bacon, one of the things they discovered was the concept of Holism. The sum of their co ordinated and concerted efforts proved to be more than the constituent parts which is still confusing as it makes no sense mathematically and yet it works. They decided on system of devision of labor that was fair and productive and continued in their quest for zero impact by installing a grey water system, composting toilet, worm farm, solar heating, wind turbines, bio gas, and an organic garden that was so prolific that the excess produce was donated to an old age home nearby and the rest sold at premium prices at the farmers market held on Saturdays just down the road past the willow tree on the left after you cross the bridge.

All this was just hunky dory and you would expect the story to end here for some reason and everyone to live happily ever after, but what about the Wolf? Would he be living happily ever after with the neighborhood having gone to pork and suffering a boiled butt in the process?

A good question and I'm glad I asked.

Now, one evening while the three Pigs were relaxing in their outdoor hot tub and they were contentedly sipping on their wheat grass shakes they heard the most unbelievable music being carried over the forest on the cool evening breeze. What on Earth could be the source of this heavenly sound they each wondered. Curiosity, not being restricted to cats and actually quite widely distributed across the entire expanse of the animal kingdom, caused them to don their finest evening clothes and some mozzie repellent and wander off in the opposite direction of the prevailing breeze. It wasn't long before they realized their mistake and did an about turn and before long they stopped abruptly as they witnessed the Wolf himself!

Sitting under a tree in the pale silvery moonlight, guitar in hand and singing the most captivating Blues you ever have heard. His voice could be described as "deep brown" but it wouldn't do him the deserved justice. Wow! He had some colors in there that you would be hard pressed to find in the entire visible spectrum! To put it plainly. The Wolf Rocked dude!

Now the Pigs being Capitalists by default and bolstered by the prospect of the all elusive profit, took no time in plucking up the collective courage to go down there and confront the Wolf.

What happened was this: They approached the Wolf and offered to specially create an annex to the "Domestead" at their own expense which they would equip with all the latest digital goodies, gizmo's and gadgets you could think of and produce the Wolf's first album. He would get royalties and after deductions all the profits would be donated to worthy charities and the Pigs would have exclusive rights to the whole of the Wolfs back catalog.

By doing so they put one of the primary principles of the so called Permaculture theory into practice and that of course would be "People care" Possibly the most important one of the lot. (The word people here is of course used metaphorically in the context of the story...or rather the Pigs and the Wolf are..Anyway, I think you get the drift)

And so, dear reader...we can now say for certain.......
...."And they *all* lived happily ever after"

End

One day revolution

I have a philosophy! Its not very complex and thats the beauty of it. Its also not all that revolutionary as its based on sound common sense.

Most Philosophers are well educated and have vocabularies as long as both my arms and an elephants memory.. They expound and compound and confound and its all very suavely done...especially if you are a suave type of Philosopher.

These guys are who you read if you're to have any cred as an intellectual and are expected to not only be familiar with the ins and outs of their confuddling jargoonisation but you're supposed to actually be able to refute or quasi accept the pseudo semi truths of their surmising. To extrapolate ever so subtly...Philosophers are cool! They're super smart and thats why smarty pants people read them and are so considered acceptably smart enough to be included in conversations by other super dooper smart people.

So a Philosophy of my own that is simple and understandable and based on commonsense things that any fool can understand is basically doomed to fail right from a little before the outset.

I don't really care though as it a philosophy that has worked for me and so I shall share it with the global population who don't really read my notes on FB and the precious few that actually do!

This is for you!

It goes a little like this....

You have 24hours in your day! Its the same everywhere. Whether you live in the Arctic Circle and have loooong days and noooo nights or the reverse...usually applies to people on the opposite pole. Bipolar people included.

If you're an average Joe...or Joline..my bet is that you spend about 7-8 hours sleeping each night with the possible exception of weekends which, if you are you're definitely average because you're BORING!!

Anyway...back to the thing here...

So ..according to a rough calculation you will be sleeping about 33% of your alloted 24 hours away. That leaves you with the rest!..Which..as time goes by you will squander by washing, shaving, brushing your teeth, eating, washing dishes, driving and a hundred and one other things that are part and parcel of living in our wonderful constantly modern world.

I haven't even gotten to the other thing that most people besides Politicians, Priests and the Unemployed do..its called WORK! I am sure you have heard of it.

So...what kind of time are *YOU* actually left with? By my calculations...almost *Nada* dude..or dudess. No offense. Its true.

So what to do?

I'm not too sure but have an idea which I will get to but only after the next little morsel of brain food..

Lets look at life as a whole..

You're born..sure..you knew that! But then straight afterwards you spent the next almost 20 years getting out of diapers, going to school, skinning your knee, falling off your bike and basically hadn't a clue about life until you got kicked out of the nest and then went to university if you were lucky and could afford it and then still didn't have a clue but were at least working towards being qualified at something that payed better than the other jobs available to others who had less of a clue than you.

Now...taking into consideration that most people only live till about 85 or so and retire at 65 or so also. It means that you work for ..mm..45 years approximately of which you sleep 33% away as agreed on beforehand..The last 20 years of your life also have the .."sleep tax" and so you are left with whatever 20 minus 33% of 20 equals..and by this stage you're far too decreppid to do much else except hang around buzzed out on Valiums waiting to break your hip.

Its a sad story..all the more because its an absolute truth for more people than you may wish to imagine. For the poor people in 3rd world countries its much much worse and of course that wont make you feel any better because you're too busy wondering when you will have to upgrade your, laptop, phone, washing machine, running shoes , golf clubs, car, 2nd car, microwave, and the ever trusty television whose intrinsic value I will summarily attempt to destroy a little later...

So the long and the short of it that you are left with very little, if any free time in your life and that goes for the duration.

What to do?

Enter my simple one day philosophy ..page left, next line..

....Make a timetable!

Who would have thought?

Basically you have to do two things.

One- make a real life timetable of what it is that you actually do.

Most people who realize that life is short and want to do something about it are already half way down the tracks at least.

The other thing is that now that you have gone halfway down said tracks you have developed all those quirky little habits along the way which serve to define your persona or whatever.

Basically you have investigate what you do before trying to institute some kind of change.

The idea would be to make one timetable for your week and another or even two for your weekend.

Once you have this you will better be able to see where you can instigate the little changes. Note I said the little changes...thats because big, drastic changes don't last more than a day or two..a week at best. You already have a lifestyle and the idea is to tweak it slightly..so you can have more *time*

How exactly do you do that?

Never sleeping again ..ever! Is one idea but it doesn't work. ....Period. ...I tried.

The first step is to not change your current one much at all. The trick is to do the overlapping activities in a ritualistic way. I hate the word ritual but the fact is that we humans are creatures of habit and thrive on set patterns of behavior.

The ritual thing is for the morning SSS routine. Some people get straight up and shower. I do. Its the only way I can wake up properly. The thing is to do your shower as if it were a seriously important ritual! Because it is. Make it like a way to achieve perfection...treat the bathroom as a sacred space. When you step into it you are in a holy space. Lets face it . It is!! you're going to get butt naked and be at your most vulnerable possibly for the whole day.

There is a lot to say about ritual and to my thinking the most important is this. You think about what you are doing while you're doing it and, coupled with a clearly set out routine you will perform better overall and free the mind to be unencumbered with peripheral thoughts.

Its a quiet time..the bathroom..maybe you sing which is a very healthy thing to do but according to my philosophy it comes at a later stage..

Once your ritual is established .. you are to pay attention to what you're doing, when you're doing it. This is the crux.

DO NOT think about work, the car, the news, ..I repeat. DO NOT! The idea is to cleanse the mind whilst the body is being cleansed.

The idea applies to other "rote" activities. Take thinking out of the equation and replace it with paying attention. Try a simple thing like making a cup of tea! It works for the Japanese and they know karate so don't knock it.

Once you have done a week or so and feel that you're getting to the point where the bathroom is going into automatic so to speak, you should then be ready to create a brand new timetable based on what your personal *needs* are in terms of personal development. Set reasonable goals. *Set reasonable goals...*

You cant eat the whole pizza in one bite..you have to make manageable slices.

In my case I am Juggling right now. I try to learn a new pattern and don't make a deadline. My goal is to *practice!* Thats it! I set aside a time to do it and have fun. There is no guilt trip, reproach. None of that. My goal is to get out there on a regular basis and if I am unable to for whatever reason then..OK tomorrow!

Maybe you play golf or some other type of competitive sport/activity. Try..and I do mean try.. to make it fun. Bugger the winning and losing! ..as you won the moment you got on the field, court, course or even in your car to go to your place of activity. You WON!

The competition should be with you alone and you can never lose if you make the benchmark for success a reasonable one and maintain a healthy perspective.

Now..There are some things you cannot change. Accept it!

There are some things you would like to and and can, so get stuck in. Small bites on a continual basis is the secret.

So you love photography. Make some time. MAKE IT!

Now that you have your " what I do list" you can see the things that steal time. Television is one of them. You DO NOT need to hear, see or read the news!! Its a want and it comes at the expense of what you could rather be doing that would make you happy. I don't ever see people happy when they have just watched the news. It a CON! It is a THIEF! Talk about something else at work. You will hear the most topical stuff there anyway and you know what? It makes not the slightest difference to your life if you know it or not! Your time can and should be better spent.

I would like to tell you to blow up your TV but that would make me a hypocrite. I LOVE movies! The difference is that I *choose* when I will watch and according to this yet to be named philosophy ..so should you! Take control of your life by not allowing that kind of stuff to control it for you.

By looking at your what I do list you can see your natural trends and rhythms. Use them! I have been saying for about 27 years solid ..I will get up at 5 am and do my meditation and training...I do..I admit it.

My success rate..Once or perhaps twice for the first two days of the week for nearly 20 years running..So..it simply doesn't work.

I am a night person. When I schedule my training sessions for after supper or even early evening. I feel really good, alive alert and do much better work. So. The lesson is...change.

If you are one of the people reading this that feels..hey! I do feel like a change because I'm not really happy then you should. Happiness is the goal.

It's a well known strategy in sports.."change a losing game!" .."don't change a winning one" If you are not happy then you need to change your game.

There is an awful lot more to say on the matter and believe me its quite awful so let me try to sum up.

One –look at what you are doing by looking at what you're doing..

Two- see how you can do more of what you want by eliminating the useless..

Three- Turn your whole life into a ritual in small consecutive and constant steps.

Four-Practice!

Five- Have fun while you're doing it.

Its not a dress rehearsal. Its your life!

Did you love *Incranium*? Then you should read *Got Change?*[1] by Jon-Pat Myers!

"It's all Johnny Rotten's fault! If I had been facing a different direction or chewing gum none of this would have happened. I might have gone on to better things and won the Nobel prize or found the cure to cancer. As it happened, I didn't do any of those things, and I place the blame squarely on the shoulders of the Sex Pistols."

Jon-Pat Myers is not a writer. He'd be the first to tell you that. This book was created using a Dictaphone, a cellphone, and an antiquated laptop. At his own request, it has not been professionally edited. It is raw. Like JP's life. Brought to you from the back alleys of Hillbrow, and from the war-torn streets of Israel.

---

1. https://books2read.com/u/4DRDgg

2. https://books2read.com/u/4DRDgg

"This is simply my story, and although I have omitted certain things for personal reasons and have refrained as much as possible from taking a particular stance in hindsight or foresight, all of it is true and I leave it to the reader to formulate their own opinions."

Read more at https://web.facebook.com/jonpat.myers.7/.

About the Author

From playing with punk legends Toxiksox in 1980s Johannesburg, to working as a roadie for Motorhead, to singing with The Psykotix and trying to kickstart disc golf in 21st century South Africa, Jon-Pat Myers has done it all.

Now he tells it his way, ranting and raving about a world he claims he cannot change.

Jon-Pat is not a writer. He'd be the first to tell you that. His books were created using a Dictaphone, a cellphone, and an antiquated laptop. At his own request, they have not been professionally edited. They are raw. Like JP's life. Brought to you from the back alleys of Hillbrow, and from the war-torn streets of Israel. Come journey with a Madman. Sculptor. Musician. Composer. Painter. Traveller. Speaker. Disc golfer. Poet. Clown. Juggler. Teacher. Student. Doorman. Gardener. Current occupation - unknown.

Read more at https://web.facebook.com/jonpat.myers.7/.

About the Publisher

We've all had those nights where drunken sex with a witch in a blood pentagram under a full moon on the roof of your favourite Johannesburg nightclub summons a hard-drinking demon who changes the fate of the human race forever. Right? No? Just me, then? ?♠? Enter Burning Books' decadent twisted world of mystery, music, magick & mayhem at www.FaceBook.com/BurningRosesNovel

www.ingramcontent.com/pod-product-compliance
Lightning Source LLC
Chambersburg PA
CBHW031318160726
47993CB00001B/460